Routledge Revivals

The Story of an Epoch Making Movement

The Story of an Epoch Making Movement

Maud Nathan

Routledge
Taylor & Francis Group

First published in 1926 by Doubleday, Page and Company

This edition first published in 2019 by Routledge
2 Park Square, Milton Park, Abingdon, Oxon, OX14 4RN
and by Routledge
52 Vanderbilt Avenue, New York, NY 10017, USA

Routledge is an imprint of the Taylor & Francis Group, an informa business

© 1926 by Taylor and Francis

Publisher's Note
The publisher has gone to great lengths to ensure the quality of this reprint b
points out that some imperfections in the original copies may be apparent.

Disclaimer
The publisher has made every effort to trace copyright holders and welcome
correspondence from those they have been unable to contact.
A Library of Congress record exists under ISBN:

ISBN 13: 978-0-367-19478-9 (hbk)
ISBN 13: 978-0-429-20270-4 (ebk)

Give back to the women who work

The Spirit of Life

Designed by Daniel Chester French for the Trask Memorial at Saratoga, and
through the courtesy of Mrs Katrina Trask, used for the leaflets of the Con
sumers' League

THE STORY OF AN EPOCH-MAKING MOVEMENT

BY

MAUD NATHAN

Honorary President of the New York
Consumers' League, and Vice-
President of the National
Consumers' League

With Brief Forewords by

HON. NEWTON D. BAKER
Former Secretary of War, and former President of
the National Consumers' League

MARY ANDERSON
Chief of Women's Bureau, Department of Labor,
Washington, D. C.

EDWARD A. FILENE
Senior member of the firm of William Filene's Sons,
of Boston, Mass.

GARDEN CITY   NEW YORK
DOUBLEDAY, PAGE & COMPANY
1926

DEDICATED TO THE MEMORY OF
MY FRIEND

JOSEPHINE SHAW LOWELL
"THE LADY OF THE LAMP"

WHOSE VISION, WISDOM, AND
SYMPATHETIC UNDERSTANDING
MADE POSSIBLE THIS EPOCH-
MAKING MOVEMENT

And for success, I ask no more than this — to bear unflinching witness to the truth. All true, whole men succeed; for what is worth success's name, unless it be the thought, the inward surety, to have carried out a noble purpose to a noble end.

— JAMES RUSSELL LOWELL

ACKNOWLEDGMENT

To the friends who so kindly encouraged me by their helpful suggestions, I wish to extend my thanks.

MAUD NATHAN

FOREWORD BY NEWTON D. BAKER

IN THE following pages Mrs. Nathan tells the story of the Consumers' League from the genesis of the idea through the days of its development to its present days of power.

The idea upon which the League is based is now an accepted part of our industrial philosophy while the League itself is relied upon by legislatures for accurate information as to industrial conditions and by executives for sympathy and support in the enforcement of regulations profoundly affecting the health and welfare of the republic.

We are a humane and just people. In recent decades, as science and invention have facilitated our exploitation of the boundless natural resources of our virgin continent, our wealth has increased in a sort of dizzy geometrical progression, but it is a happy circumstance that our disposition to benevolence has kept pace with our growing ability. I shall not multiply words in proof of this thesis, but I summon the four corners of the earth to testify how American effort has bound up the wounds of the world, pouring in oil and wine, until the advent of catastrophe has come to be but the herald of the approach of American sympathy and relief.

The industrial advance, however, has entailed problems all its own. In the surging, congested masses, notably of unorganized and inarticulate women and children workers, summoned to create wealth in mass production, it is increasingly hard for us to find our neighbours! The Providence which lay in the intimacy of small neighbourhoods is lost in the mazes of the tenement, and charity becomes unintelligent and futile as a mere casual grace between strangers. For such reasons the factory and workshop, as they grew, became more and more impersonal, conditions in them became nobody's business, and their social consequences eluded the knowledge of the consumers of the products until the exhaustion of long hours, the degradation of inadequate wages and the diseases of the sweatshop stood out as evils which not only deprived defenceless women and children of a fair chance in life, but menaced the vitality and morality of the race.

The attention of Miss Woodbridge was attracted to some of these problems through the Working Women's Society, an organization dictated, no doubt, rather by the consciousness of suffering on the part of the working women than by any appreciation of the social consequences of the condition in which they and other women found themselves.

However that may be, a Cause had finally found a Prophet. By the steps which Mrs. Nathan details, the Consumers' League developed at first locally, then nationally. It assumed, and rightly, that the American consumer would not willingly profit by the cheapness of wares where that cheapness resulted from oppression and injustice. Happily, from the very beginning, however, the Consumers' League has proceeded upon sound principles. Its motto has been "Investigate, record, agitate." Accordingly, it has sought first-hand accurate information, subjected its data to scientific analysis and generalization, and laid before a thoughtful public the results of its inquiries, through the printed and spoken word, in such fashion that well-disposed people have been able to bring to bear the pressure of the consumers' purchasing power to induce voluntary betterment of conditions on the part of employers. It has been able also to present before legislative committees conditions ripe for statutory remedies, and to hold up the hands of factory inspectors and sanitary authorities by surrounding their acts with an atmosphere of intelligent criticism.

The full story of the work of the Consumers' League is not told in Mrs. Nathan's pages, nor will it ever be told anywhere. Before local and general legislatures of every state, and committees of Congress, in the offices of mayors, governors, cabinet officers, and Presidents, the voice of the League has been lifted in the interest of better conditions of life and work, notably for women and children. The impression it has created has become a part of the elevation of the social conscience of America and far transcends even the great ethical gains which can be enumerated as embodied in legislation.

In a peculiar sense the Consumers' League is an ideal voluntary agency evolved in an industrial democracy. For the most part, laws are needed only for recalcitrants. Spontaneous good behaviour, dictated by good will and enforced by common consent, makes up the larger part of the sanction of civilized life. Such spontaneous good behaviour can rest only upon knowledge of the implications of conduct, and knowledge can only be acquired, under modern conditions, when high-minded and disinterested inquirers investigate and tell us what they find. This sort of work the Consumers' League has done supremely well in a field in which it was a pioneer.

There is a certain reassurance, too, in the story Mrs. Nathan tells. A small and obscure beginning grows by the very *vis inertia* of our democratic institutions into a great social agency as the need for it develops. We are not likely to become a mere materialistic society, however much the complications of modern life may thwart our ability as individuals to practise the charitable virtues, so long as associations like the Consumers' League can develop and thrive among us and help us to do on a large and collective scale, in a collective way, that which we so delighted to do as individuals under simpler conditions.

FOREWORD BY MARY ANDERSON

IN READING Mrs. Nathan's book, I have lived again the hard, lean days, with their long hours and low pay, which women have had to endure through the ages. And the end is not yet.

Three things must strike forcibly the readers of this book. One is the deplorable condition of women workers in retail stores, which led to the founding of the Consumers' League. Another is the progress recorded —progress so gratifying that the Consumers' League and its members may well be proud of having had so large a part in the work. And though much has been accomplished, much remains to be done. The third is the unbounding faith and untiring effort of women who had nothing to gain and—I suspect—frequently were misunderstood, both by those they were trying to help and by the employer, the latter too often of the type which considers that the business, including the human element, is his to do with as he likes.

A book such as this of Mrs. Nathan's, which gives us the history of a constructive movement, is very helpful in the review of our industrial life. In the dark days we need a clear vision and a well-grounded hope, and that calm courage which takes no account of hardships by the way. The times through which we are passing are affording to many of us a confirmation of our faith.

We see that many things are evil, and through that knowledge we know more definitely than we ever did before the direction in which we must move if a better world is to come.   The Consumers' League has had and will continue to have an important part in forming our industrial democracy.

FOREWORD BY EDWARD A. FILENE

THE history of the Consumers' League is a record of real achievement. The League has accomplished in large measure the fundamental purposes for which it was organized, and it would be difficult, if not impossible, to find in any department store to-day the deplorable conditions that Mrs. Nathan has so graphically described.

Two conclusions may be drawn from her book. The League's success shows that the consumer can exert a decisive influence over business, if he will take the trouble. And it shows that the time has come to discard some of our present more or less lawless business methods and to adopt the sort of policies that will give us an increasingly better social order.

Mrs. Nathan's book is the description of a long and successful struggle. But Mrs. Nathan and her associates will agree with me that the work of the Consumers' League is not yet done. I believe that there is more work for it still to do and, if anything, a greater work than it has already done.

The League has effectively fought one set of abuses affecting a limited class of workers. It should now set itself to eliminate the wastes in production and distribution of our modern business system. Despite the fact that science is daily making life more livable and inter-

esting, daily devising ways and means for shifting bur-
dens from the backs of men to the backs of machines,
daily widening the range of men's interests by rapid
transportation and communication, and broadening the
scope of existence generally, the time of the majority of
mankind is still occupied almost entirely in the business
of providing food, clothing, and shelter, with little time
or training for lifting life to a higher level—even if the
means were at hand.

According to Mr. Hoover's Board of Engineers in
their report on "Waste in Industry," the average pre-
ventable waste in American production reaches 50 per
cent. Distribution conditions are equally bad. The
average product doubles in price from the production
cost to the ultimate consumer. These wastes are inde-
fensible if they are to be accepted as the inevitable result
of the business system. A system that does this cannot
escape indictment and assault. And yet I am convinced that the social progress of the future will be
achieved not by the destruction of the business system,
but by its further and finer development. The pressure
of necessity during the next ten or twenty years will
enforce its reform, but the Consumers' League and the
consuming public which it represents can exert an important influence in hastening these developments.

As an instance of the consumer's influence on distribution, let me point out that if consumers will make it a
rule to shop before they purchase, so as to make certain
they are getting the best values—that is, the best articles at the lowest prices—they will save their own
money and they will help to better the methods of pro-

duction and distribution in American business. The distributor's best and most real service consists in selling goods of reliable quality, made under just conditions, at increasingly lower prices. There is a prevailing idea that there is something petty in trying to find the best for the lowest price, and that it is an evidence of superiority to buy without questioning whatever is shown. But to do that is to lend support to those costlier methods of production and distribution which are so largely responsible for the high cost of living, so largely responsible for making food, clothing, and shelter take up so large a share of the average income that there is little left for education and the other spiritual values of life.

If the Consumers' League can bring home to its members and the buying public in general the idea that when they insist on the best value each time they buy, they will be performing one of the services our country needs most, the League will add a new field to its usefulness. They will show that their work has a direct and important bearing not only on the economic progress, but also on the political and social progress of the world, and even on its spiritual progress.

In the final analysis beauty is the greatest objective of the world. ·But we cannot teach spiritual truths effectively to starving people. One great way to make more beauty in this world is to make the obtaining of a living—the obtaining of the necessary food, clothing, and shelter, and the necessary minimum of luxuries— so mechanical and so little time-consuming that we all shall have time for avocations—have time to work for and search for better things—to search for beauty. This can be accomplished by saving of waste, by more economic justice, by invention and better organization of production and distribution, by better training of workers and leaders.

Because Mrs. Nathan's book points out how effective the work of the Consumers' League has been in the past, I believe that a greater work awaits them in helping to make the modern business system an instrument of social progress. It is that idea which I have sought to emphasize in these few lines.

CONTENTS

THE STORY OF AN
EPOCH–MAKING MOVEMENT

THE STORY OF
AN EPOCH–MAKING MOVEMENT

CHAPTER I

LOOKING BACKWARDS

I heard a trumpet blown beyond the hills
And, riding forth, I found a host of men
Roused by summons.
—Bernard Drew.

I lifted up my hands to find
A lamp amid the darkness.
—Omar Khayyám.

THIRTY-FIVE years ago the traveller arriving on a Saturday afternoon in July or August in the great metropolis of the greatest republic in the world, would have found a great, throbbing, pulsing crowd wending its way in and out of the huge hives of industry which opened wide their inviting doors on Broadway, along Fourteenth Street, Twenty-third Street, and on Sixth Avenue between these two streets. Not all the people were bent on making purchases; a few of them may really have been looking for articles which they required; many, however, were searching in a desultory way for some article which at some future time they might possibly require; a large majority were amusing themselves by wandering about looking at the pretty wares displayed, and enjoying themselves with no expense involved. But was there no expense involved? None, apparently, for the shoppers; the clerks, however, were paying, perhaps, with their flesh and blood for the innocent amusement. For from seven forty-five in the morning until after eleven at night, with only a short time allowed for meals, they were expected to stand behind counters, smile on would-be customers, and cajole them into buying what they didn't want, if the article asked for didn't happen to be in stock.

In the evening the lights in the stores made them more alluring than ever to the passersby, who were out strolling to get a breath of fresh air; many would walk in one door, swell the crowd, exhaust some of the vanishing oxygen of the air in the store, handle the goods, ask prices (ignorant of the old Talmudic adage that to price an article with no intention of buying it was a crime),[1] and then proceed to walk around and out of another door.

When the closing gong finally sounded, the loiterers had to be almost pushed out of the stores. Then counters had to be cleared and covered, stock put in order, and at last weary limbs automatically carried the clerks down to sub-basements, where, after some confusion in the dimly lighted partitions, hats and wraps were found. To be accurate, they were not always

---

[1]Claude Montefiore, in his book, "The Old Testament and After," quotes from the Mishnah to show that "One must not ask the price of an article if one does not intend to buy it"—"If one has no money one must not look at the goods in a shop."

found; scarfs and gloves, umbrellas and rubbers, and occasionally a good sontag mysteriously disappeared. There were no individual lockers, and when an article was stolen, the only result seemed to be that the girl who made the complaint lost her position as well as the article. The girls considered themselves lucky if they were able to find all their belongings and pass out into the street without being told to return the following morning (Sunday) to "take stock" or to help rearrange stock which was to be moved to another department.

There were always some youths and older men waiting at the back doors of the mercantile establishments to escort the girls home or to entice them elsewhere. There may have been a few girls so fatigued that their morale being weakened they more easily succumbed to temptation, but the vast majority of them went directly to their homes. There was housework or laundry work to be done, and not until this was accomplished could they crawl into bed, to rest their aching feet and backs, even though the heat might prevent them from sleeping. Many of the workers lived in the congested districts, where there seemed to be great waves of humanity which, on hot nights, surged backwards and forwards, climbing fire escapes to roofs, clambering back to stifling little rooms, gasping for air, tossing about in search of slumber that they were eager to snatch before starting another day of discomfort.

During the periods of scorching days in July and August in New York, the sun rises red and torrid, pitiless in a cloudless sky; bricks and stone pavements seem almost to sizzle under its blazing rays, and there is no respite from the glare and humidity for several successive days. Yet the shop-girl, thirty-five years ago, didn't ask for a vacation, for vacations in those days meant vacations without pay, and those who needed them most were those who received the lowest wage and were therefore ill-nourished and anæmic. Vacations, shady lawns, cool breezes, surf bathing—these were luxuries to be enjoyed only by the residents of the uptown districts where row after row of closed brownstone houses proclaimed the owners to be away.

But was the vision of a summer outing the only thing that haunted the imagination of the salesgirl? What were the working conditions of other seasons? The heat and oppressiveness of the stores in midsummer were more easily borne than the vitiated air of basements in midwinter. Added to this discomfort were the confusion, the impatience, the rudeness of the dense, pushing throngs of shoppers during the rush, the hurry of the so-called holiday season: Christmas, the season of cheer and good will! At this period hours were prolonged until close on to midnight. "Extra Junior Salesgirls"—often employed only during this season of stress—were seen time and again shivering and weeping at street corners after midnight, waiting for a street car to take them to their homes in outlying districts. Hours on Saturdays throughout the year were intolerably long. Stores were kept open late at night to enable the wife of the working man to do her shopping after her husband had taken his weekly pay envelope to her. Workers in various industries were also enabled to do their purchasing after their own working hours were over.

It is not so many years since the proprietor of a small store in Saco, Maine, had the temerity to engage a "female clerk." It created quite a stir among the gossips of the village. Some of the more conservative element refused to condone such a scandalous procedure. They said it was unethical to place a woman in such a public position, where she was obliged to converse with any stranger who saw fit to enter the store; indeed, it would give the store a bad name, and men of evil repute would flock to it. So the respectable women clutched their skirts and crossed the way, preferring to make their purchases elsewhere.

Years later hundreds of girls worked in stores. It took a long time to adjust matters to meet the new conditions. No one had thought of providing seats behind counters for male clerks; they were considered strong enough to stand on their feet all day; yet the exigencies of salesmanship did not require this undue strain. When, instead of men, women, generally conceded to belong to the frailer sex, began in larger and larger numbers to serve as clerks, even then employers saw no necessity to provide seats. Customers, although only in the stores for a short period of time, were provided with stools, but these were screwed to the floor in front of counters and so could not be utilized by the saleswomen. Indeed, clerks were not permitted even to bring up boxes from basements to sit upon. If they did this surreptitiously, the boxes were removed the following day. If they pulled out a drawer at the

back of the counter, and sat on its edge, they were rebuked by the floor-walker; if they leaned on the front
counter, they were told it looked unbusinesslike and
that a straight posture was required.

Girls were known to faint occasionally; when this
happened they were stretched out on the concrete
floor of the retiring room, and if they did not recover
rapidly, they were sent home and their pay envelopes
suffered in consequence. For in those days there were
no well-equipped rest rooms or trained nurses to attend
to their needs. No consideration was paid to aching
feet and aching backs; a smiling face to greet the customer and a pleasant remark were expected, no matter
what the physical discomfort might be.

It was an unwritten law that a saleswoman who did
not stand erect all day long, but who was occasionally
seen slouching or leaning on something, should merit a
rebuke. When there was no customer to be served, if
she did not simulate occupation, such as arranging
stock, dusting the counter, or making the display of
goods look more attractive, she would find before long
that her services would be dispensed with. Indeed, a
saleswoman's duty was to persuade a customer to
buy something else, should the article she asked for not
be in stock; if she permitted a customer to leave the
counter without making a purchase, she would receive a
reprimand.

There was no special duration of time accorded for
the luncheon hour; twenty minutes was *supposed* to be
the rule, but during the rush season saleswomen were
advised to take but ten minutes for their frugal repast,

in order that they might return as quickly as possible to wait on customers. Each saleswoman was *supposed* to have a specific time for luncheon, but if one happened to be busy waiting on a customer, she was obliged to postpone her lunch hour. However, if she remained away from the counter after the time she was due to return, she was apt to be rebuked by the floor-walker. For instance, in a department where there were but two or three clerks and one absent for any cause, the luncheon time might be so encroached upon that often a salesgirl would be unable to snatch a bite before three o'clock; it was not unknown for her to skip her luncheon entirely, because of the rush of custom and the lack of sufficient saleswomen.

Floor-walkers in the old days were veritable tsars; they often ruled with a rod of iron. Only the girls who were "free-and-easy" with them, who consented to lunch or dine with them, who permitted certain liberties, were allowed any freedom of action, or felt secure in their positions. Rules in regard to leaving the counter were in some instances so rigid that the health of the saleswomen was apt to be impaired. Sometimes, rather than ask permission of the floor-walker to retire, they would use repression which involved physical suffering. In some instances permission to leave the counter was denied. A complaint lodged against a floor-walker or against the head of a department—superior officers—was almost invariably followed by dismissal of the one who had made the complaint.

So little trust was placed in the ethical behaviour of saleswomen that, in some of the large department stores, no privacy was accorded them in their retiring rooms. Doors were taken down from toilets, and not even a curtain was put up to replace them, the explanation being that if the saleswomen were concealed, they might remain away from their work an inordinately long time. The women's toilets were often adjoining those of the men, with very meagre partitions between them. The doors were frequently side by side. In some of the smaller stores, there was but one toilet for both sexes. Often the dressing rooms were partitioned off from the lunch rooms, and these were found in dark basements, without sufficient light and air, and with plumbing conditions so appalling as to endanger the health of the employees. In one department store, the so-called lunch room was merely a corner of the retiring room in a sub-cellar. There was no window, and flickering gas jets were consuming whatever little air was there. Leaking pipes from the toilets made the concrete floor so wet that planks were laid on the floor; a large packing box in the centre of the space was utilized as a table, and smaller wooden boxes served as seats. Permission was given for the employees to go out for luncheon, but this meant consumption of time and money; it was cheaper to bring their lunch from home.

The two great holidays of the Christian year Christmas and Easter—imposed upon the workers hardships which to-day seem incredible. If the hours for salesgirls and cash girls seemed long, what can be said of the hours for cashiers, packers, and delivery clerks? The cashiers were often young girls recently graduated from high schools. Their work entailed a great deal of bookkeeping and the making out of many detailed accounts. Long after the stores were closed, they could have been seen (had shades not been carefully drawn) poring over their books, in order to have bills correctly made out by the beginning of the month. In the basements the huge mounds of gifts purchased had to be packed and delivered even at a late hour, in order to avoid too much congestion during the last overcrowded days. On each delivery wagon there was a small boy with the driver, so that his young, lithe limbs could enable him the more nimbly to run up and down steps and deliver bundles the more rapidly. Christmas gifts had to be delivered before Christmas no matter how dilatory the purchasers had been. On Christmas Eve there were always a large number of deliveries to be made, some of them at a great distance from the stores. For suburban deliveries, there were relays of horses for the wagons, but no relays of drivers or of delivery boys! It was known that one little fellow was so exhausted when the last package had been delivered in a home (where the inmates had retired for the night and had to be aroused in order to receive it) that he fell asleep before the trip was over. When the driver returned to the barn at 3 A. M. to unharness the horse, he pulled a horse blanket over the little fellow, and in pity heeded his plea to let him sleep on. The next morning the driver returned to the barn and found the little chap frozen to death. The joyous Christmas chimes pealed his funeral dirge.

Life's little ironies were also enacted at Thanksgiving time. In one of the department stores where delicacies were sold for Thanksgiving feasts, a young fellow in the packing department was kept steadily at work from 8 A. M. until 4 A. M. the following morning (a working day of twenty hours), with only sufficient time off to enable him to get something to eat and drink. He had to return at 8 A.·M. to complete the packing for the feast which occurred the following day. Surely he was able to give thanks from the depths of his heart for the legal holiday which permitted him to rest at home for twenty-four hours. Legal holidays, however, were not a cause for rejoicing, as a rule, to store employees; for their pay envelopes were reduced whenever these occurred.

At the Easter season, it was not the saleswomen who dreaded that holiday, since in olden days Easter gifts were not so customary as at present; it was the girls who worked in the millinery and dressmaking departments who realized that hats and gowns had to be completed, no matter how late the orders had been given, and no matter how late they had to stay to complete them.

Wages were low because salesmanship in the old days was considered unskilled labour. Girls without experience were placed behind counters and expected to learn, from the other girls, selling tactics and the method of keeping their books. There were no schools of salesmanship and no standards of employment. Wages were so low that some firms refused to employ young girls unless they lived at home, for they knew full well that no one could afford to pay for board and lodging on the meagre salary received. So, many an applicant, in order to obtain a position, pretended to live at home, and in reality half starved herself so as to be able to pay for a roof over her head. It was the policy of one well-known firm with branches all over the country, to pay their salesgirls two dollars a week. When an applicant for a position stated that she could not possibly live on such a small sum, she was told by the manager of the store where she had applied that there were other ways of eking out her income!

In the old days there were no special hotels or boarding houses for working girls; when a girl was obliged to seek a very low-priced room, she was forced either to go to a disreputable locality or take unsanitary, dark, shabby quarters, or else go to the suburbs and pay extra carfare, or share her room with one or two others.

Nearly all the leading stores had a system of fines which frequently reduced the already extremely low wage to a still lower level. For instance, whereas stock-taking and rearrangement of stock had to be done after store hours without pay for overtime (a light supper was sometimes given, by way of compensation), yet if salesgirls were more than five minutes late in arriving the next morning after such extra duty, they were fined. In some stores and factories, if they were more than fifteen minutes late, they were obliged to lose a half day's pay. The chief hardship consisted in the fact that in some establishments the doors were closed on the girls; they were not allowed to enter until after the noon hour. This rule necessitated their walking the streets, often in stormy weather, as tardiness was

frequently caused by snowstorms and poor traffic conditions, or by ferry boats being delayed. Many of the
girls lived too far away to return home and did not
wish, moreover, to pay double carfare. Fines were
also imposed for infraction of other rules, and for
damaging, losing, or breaking articles in stock. One
little cash-girl was fined for knocking off a vase which
had been placed too near the edge of a counter. Her pay
envelope at the end of the week contained, therefore,
but twenty-five cents—not sufficient for the carfare
she had expended in order to reach the store before
8 A. M.

Thirty-five years ago there were few opportunities
for the girls to get to the country. Moreover, since no
vacations were granted with pay, the mere thought of a
vacation was a nightmare. They dreaded being told
that they could take a vacation; it meant practically
a suspension of salary, and that meant that they
would have to look for a temporary job in order to keep
body and soul together. Vacations without pay were
accorded lavishly; for the employer it meant a cutting
down of expenses. Many customers went away for
the entire summer and fewer employees were required.
The girls who worked in the millinery departments
were frankly told that they were "laid off." The millinery seasons were very short—a few weeks in the
spring, and again in the autumn. Milliners found it
necessary to learn two trades in order to keep the wolf
from the door. More than once, clerks in mercantile
establishments endeavoured to form a union in order
to protect themselves against exploitation, but em-

ployers were very much opposed to this, and threatened to dismiss any clerk who joined any union.

In the old days the interests of employers and employees were considered antagonistic; there was no spirit of coöperation; employers had not learned that even for selfish reasons it is wiser to give their employees good working conditions; that for their own benefit, for the sake of securing better service, it is good policy to raise industrial standards.

As for the general public—the customers who frequented the stores—they were indifferent and selfish. They were entirely oblivious of the needs or discomfort of those who served them from the other side of the counters. It was not that women thirty-five years ago were cruel or inhuman: they were merely thoughtless and careless. The New York society woman drove up and down Fifth Avenue and Broadway; then, before going up to take a turn around Central Park, dropped in casually at Arnold, Constable's or Lord & Taylor's to see what novelties were displayed on the counters. If, after having bolt after bolt opened for her to look at, she found some material which pleased the eye, she had sufficient for a gown sent home. If the family dressmaker disapproved, or if she happened to find something she liked better in some other store, she knew she could return it and have it credited to her account. The firm might charge her for a quarter of a yard, and then sell the goods as a remnant. If Milady looked at mantillas or bonnets, she would have them sent home, copied, and then ask the firm to send for them and have them credited. She would boast of her shrewd economies and show with pride the garment or the headgear which she had copied from an imported article and through the efforts of the home dressmaker had secured at a bargain price! This was not considered unethical, it was astute. What would clerks do all day in a store if patrons didn't keep them occupied showing their wares? What were merchants for, if not to cater to customers who had accounts at their stores? Milady lolled back in her victoria, with never a thought of the saleswomen standing all day behind counters, or for the merchant trying to earn an honest living, greatly hampered by competition that was sometimes unfair. Milady had no conscientious scruples, no regrets, no compunctions. The shopping public had not been educated; the social conscience of the general public had not yet been awakened. How was the shopping public educated? How was the social conscience of the general public aroused, developed, and crystallized? It is with the view of answering these questions that the telling of this story has been undertaken.

CHAPTER II

A high end in the community is an impulse which individuals can hardly withstand. Whatever the community demands will be done.
—WILLIAM ELLERY CHANNING.

THE Working Women's Society was the forerunner
of the Women's Trade Union League. The members met in a dingy room in an old-fashioned house in
Clinton Place, New York City. This house had been
one of the fashionable residences in earlier days. Here
were discussed some of the abominable conditions
under which women wage-earners were obliged to work.
The secretary of the society, Alice Woodbridge, was
somewhat older than were the majority of the members,
and her experience had been varied and interesting.
She was slender, pale, anæmic-looking; her blue eyes
held an expression of timidity and fear. The glowing
mass of her Titian red hair served to emphasize the pal-
lor of her face and the depth of expression in her eyes.
This startling effect brought to her many offers from
artists to pose as a model. These offers, however, she
always declined, because in those days the profession
of a model was considered questionable. She had held
at various times positions in offices; these positions
had promised to be lucrative, but because of insulting

proposals from employers she had been obliged to give them up; she had been buffeted about for many a year, trying to earn an honest living and trying to live on the low wages offered her.

Alice Woodbridge was the moving force and guiding spirit of the Working Women's Society; it was her purpose to endeavour to shield other working girls from the hideous experiences which had been hers, in her efforts to live an honest, upright, independent life. Many of the members of the Working Women's Society had been recruited from department stores; they talked of the abuses they were forced to put up with; they told of incidents which occurred from time to time.

Alice Woodbridge realized how helpless were the working girls themselves to remedy conditions. She had the vision to perceive that these abuses could be abolished only if the women who patronized the stores knew about them. The supply of girls eager to serve behind counters—even at a wage which in reality was but pin money—was far larger than the demand. Therefore, whenever a girl complained about some specific abuse, she was told that if she did not like conditions as she found them, there were plenty of other girls ready to fill her place.

So, during the winter of 1889-90, Alice Woodbridge and some of her co-workers decided to make a careful study of the leading department stores; a report of the facts obtained by the investigation was written. Then Miss Woodbridge cast her eyes about for some public-spirited women who would listen to the reading of the report. She knew that Mrs. Josephine Shaw

Lowell was active in relieving the distress of the poverty-stricken and unfortunate. Mrs. Lowell had been widowed young, her husband having been one of the early victims of the Civil War. Her brother, Robert Gould Shaw, had been the colonel of the first coloured regiment which had enlisted. She spent her days trying to lessen suffering and distress. The spirit of her New England ancestors dwelt within her. Whenever a grievous wrong was brought to her attention, she felt impelled to do her share to have it righted.

To have such a character at the head of a humanitarian movement was to insure its success. Mrs. Lowell's sense of civic duty and responsibility was a source of inspiration to those who worked with her. Her example of zeal and unstinted energy compelled others to endeavour to do their share of the work to be done. Moreover, her sweet simplicity, her rigid code of ethics, her lack of self-aggrandizement endeared her to those who were fortunate enough to have been brought within her circle.

Mrs. Lowell was the founder and guiding spirit of the Charity Organization Society; she was the first woman to become an active member of the State Board of Charities, having been appointed by Governor Tilden in 1876, and remaining on the board thirteen and a half years. She had borne a leading part in securing the separation of charities and corrections; in promoting state reformatories for women, state custodial care for adult idiots, state asylums for feeble-minded women and girls; municipal lodging houses for men; and later she was instrumental in placing matrons in police stations. She gave much time to the care of dependent children, and worked to promote means leading to the suppression of the social evil. She was interested in trying to bring about industrial conciliation and arbitration.

It was to this woman that Alice Woodbridge made her appeal; to her she went with her story, and found a sympathetic listener. Notwithstanding her many activities, Mrs. Lowell did not turn a deaf ear to Alice Woodbridge's pleadings. Mrs. Lowell realized at once that here was another wrong to be righted. Without considering whether she could possibly spare the time and strength from her other duties, she took up the task at once, with the spirit of a crusader. Upon learning of the unsanitary conditions which prevailed in some of the stores, she suggested that Dr. Mary Putnam Jacobi be also shown the report.

Dr. Mary Putnam Jacobi was the daughter of the well-known publisher, George P. Putnam. She was one of the most distinguished women physicians, and was as well known professionally as her distinguished husband, Dr. Abraham Jacobi. She was the first woman to become a member of the New York Academy of Medicine, and was sent as a delegate from that body to a congress of the State Medical Association. She was also the first woman admitted to the École de Médicine, Paris. She had won the Boylston prize at Harvard University, and had been for ten years a professor at the Woman's Medical College of the New York Infirmary. She was also later known as one of the prominent leaders of the woman suffrage movement.

Mrs. Lowell and Doctor Jacobi called a small group of women together to discuss the survey and report of working conditions in retail stores as presented by Alice Woodbridge. They met in the room on Clinton Place, the headquarters of the Working Women's Society.

Mrs. Lowell asked me to go with her; she no doubt felt impelled to arouse the interest of younger women in the problems of life which would be theirs to solve at a later day. I went with Mrs. Lowell to this meeting with an unprepared mind, not knowing what I was to hear. I was but a young married woman at that time, leading the normal life of the average young woman of the leisure class of thirty-five years ago. I was interested in my husband, my little girl, my home. Only in relation to them and to the wider family circle did I recognize any duties or responsibilities. I had no conception at that time of the wider knowledge which came to me later, that a woman's duty and responsibility are not bounded by the four walls of her home. If she be capable of performing these duties with courage and initiative, of bearing the responsibilities with fortitude and poise, these strong forces belong not alone to herself to be used solely for the benefit of her loved ones, they also belong to the world outside the sheltering walls of home, and must be used for the benefit of others in the community. Every department of the home is but a reflection in miniature of the broader departments of the municipality and the world beyond. This thought did not come to me until later, and at the time I attended the meeting I might well have been the prototype of the careless, conscienceless society woman whose picture I tried to give in the preceding chapter.

Alice Woodbridge, with her fawn-like eyes, her halo of golden-red hair, sat facing the group of strange, aloof women. She told them of the wearily long hours of work, of the lack of compensation for work done after the working day was supposed to be over; she described the unsanitary surroundings; she touched upon the pitifully young children who were sometimes employed at tasks far beyond their physical strength; she related how fidelity and length of service often met only the reward of dismissal; she spoke of the low wages reduced by a system of excessive fines; she told of the physical collapse of many girls after two years of steady work, because of the long hours of standing.

These facts proved startling. None of the listeners had ever dreamed that women and children working in retail stores were often obliged to work under conditions injurious to health and morals.

The reading of that report[1] seemed to open up a new vista of life for me. Heretofore, when I had shopped for a bit of lace, I had not realized that the saleswoman had been on her feet all day long, lifting heavy boxes; when I had run into a store at a quarter before six, to purchase some trivial toilet accessory, I had not considered that I was keeping the saleswoman from arranging her counter for the closing hour, and thus detaining her unnecessarily. It flashed through my mind that I had often been inconsiderate, unsympathetic, impatient.

[1]See Appendix A for extracts from Report.

Alice Woodbridge's simple, straightforward recital of facts aroused us all to sympathetic indignation. After a heated discussion she had the satisfaction of seeing her object accomplished, for we decided to call a mass meeting. Miss Woodbridge was asked to condense her report, omitting all names of firms, and read it at the meeting. This mass meeting was held on the evening of May 6, 1890, at Chickering Hall, corner of Fifth Avenue and Eighteenth Street, under the auspices of many leading clergymen of various denominations and many prominent men and women. The public was invited to meet "to consider the condition of working women in New York retail stores." The response was greater than we had dared anticipate. The New York *Times*, in its report of the meeting printed in its issue of the following day, mentioned that the attendance was "gratifyingly large." Hon. Everett P. Wheeler, the prominent lawyer and publicist, presided, Archibald Sessions acting as secretary. Reverend Doctor Huntington of Grace Church spoke on the long hours of labour; Reverend Doctor Faunce of the Fifth Avenue Baptist Church spoke on the lack of sanitary conditions. The other speakers were Reverend Doctor Alexander, Presbyterian Church, Fifth Avenue and Tenth Street; Reverend Father Elliot, Monsignor Ducey of St. Leo's Church, and Reverend D. de Sola Mendes of Congregation Shaaray Tefila.

As I write, that picture of thirty-five years ago comes vividly to my mind. The sensation of the evening was the reading of Alice Woodbridge's report. When the chairman called upon her, she came forward quietly, timidly, and faced the large, fashionable, and representative audience. There was a hush in the auditorium; there was almost a gasp, as the frail, ethereal-looking woman began, in a subdued voice, the reading of the indictment which was destined to start an epoch-making movement.

To-day we are accustomed to hear the pleas of working women from the platform, or through the press, but thirty-five years ago it was unheard-of; as I think of it now I am amazed at the courage, the self-confidence, the sense of wrongs to be righted, which impelled this humble little woman to be the pioneer of a cause. After the report was read, resolutions were passed. The Board of Health was asked to take cognizance of the bad sanitary conditions in some of the big stores in New York. The legislature was asked to take action to fix the hours of saleswomen. Clergymen and editors were called upon to help the salesgirls improve their conditions of employment. Then followed the important resolution which was the forerunner of the Consumers' League:

Resolved that a committee be appointed to assist the Working Women's Society in making a list which shall keep shoppers informed of such shops as deal justly with their employees, and so bring public opinion and public action to bear in favour of just employers, and also in favour of such employers as desire to be just, but are prevented by the stress of competition, from following their own sense of duty.

Thus was launched a movement in the new world which was destined to mould public opinion all the world over, and which, in the estimation of Professor

Cummings of the Department of Economics at Harvard University, was one of the most important movements of the day. It was in line with the thought of the leading economists of the time. Hobson, author of "Evolution in Capitalism," had proclaimed that the wealth of a nation could be increased far more rapidly by educating consumers than by increasing the work of producers.

The joint committee appointed by the Working Women's Society and the chairman of the mass meeting decided to form an association similar in principle to one which had been organized in England during the same year. The London society had issued a statement which in its essentials expressed succinctly the motives and objects of the founders of the New York committee.[1] The English society did not thrive, however, as I shall relate in a succeeding chapter.

It was felt that conditions could only be changed through enlisting the sympathy and interest of the shopping public. Indirectly, we, the shoppers, were the employers of these girls, who were paid to stand behind the counters and serve us. Therefore, we had a direct moral responsibility toward them. We felt we could do no better than use the name already adopted by the London society (formed a few months previously): "The Consumers' League." This name, while it expressed our ideals and object, apparently created confusion in the minds of the public. Some of the merchants feared that the prime object of a consumers' league was to obtain goods at a discount;

[1]See Appendix B for statement.

later on, when I made speeches in the interest of the League, and used the words, "production, distribution, consumption," some of my hearers were known to ask how a league interested in "consumption" had for its champion such a robust, vigorous-looking leader! It was suggested that we call ourselves "The Buyers' League," but we felt that this name might conflict with a commercial organization.

In the early years we were constantly called upon to explain what a "consumers' league" meant, whereas to-day it would be difficult to find any one of ordinary intelligence who has not some knowledge, however vague or slight, of the movement.

In 1898, we considered it advisable to become an incorporated body, as other organizations with entirely different aims were using our name to further their own purposes.[1]

This initial meeting, as I have before said, was held May 6, 1890, but it was not until January 21, 1891, that the committee had actually completed its work of organization. For during the months immediately following the mass meeting, the members of this newly formed committee had scattered for their summer holiday, and while they could not be considered hard-hearted or callous, they did not feel a sufficient urge to impel them to renounce their holiday in order to hasten the instituting of contemplated reforms. The girls could swelter in stifling shops, they could pant for a cooling breath of salt air or an invigorating mountain breeze, or long to rest their tired eyes on a bit of

---
[1] See Appendix C for list of incorporators.

mossy green, while we, who were enjoying all this unthinkingly, taking this refreshment of body and soul as a matter of course and as merely incident to the season, postponed all action until the bracing autumn days.

After spending many weeks in the work of organization, the committee finally elected its officers. Mrs. Josephine Shaw Lowell accepted the presidency; Mrs. Charles A. Spofford was elected treasurer, Miss Louise Caldwell secretary, while I was asked to serve on the Board of Directors.[1]

The committee adopted a constitution which embodied the following articles:

PRINCIPLES

(1) That the interest of the community demands that all workers should receive, not the lowest wages, but fair living wages.

(2) That the responsibility for some of the worst evils from which wage-earners suffer rests with the consumers, who persist in buying in the cheapest market, regardless of how cheapness is brought about.

(3) That it is, therefore, the duty of consumers to find out under what conditions the articles which they purchase are produced, and to insist that these conditions shall be at least decent, and consistent with a respectable existence on the part of the workers.

(4) That this duty is especially incumbent upon consumers in relation to the products of woman's work, since there is no limit beyond which the wages of women may not be pressed down, unless artificially maintained at a living rate by combinations, either of the workers themselves or of consumers.

OBJECT

Recognizing the fact that the majority of employers are virtually helpless to improve conditions as to hours and wages, unless sustained by public opinion, by law, and by the action of consumers,

[1] See Appendix D for first published list of officers and governing board.

the Consumers' League declares its object to be to ameliorate the condition of the women and children employed in the retail mercantile houses of New York City, by patronizing, so far as practicable, only such houses as approach in their conditions to the "Standard of a Fair House," as adopted by the League, and by other methods.

WHITE LIST

The Advisory Board shall be required to prepare a list of retail mercantile houses which, in their opinion, should be patronized by the members of the Consumers' League, which list shall be known as the "White List," and shall be published at stated intervals in the daily papers.

MEMBERSHIP

The condition of membership shall be the approval by signature of the object of the Consumers' League, and all persons shall be eligible for membership excepting such as are engaged in retail business in New York (either as employer or employee).

The members shall not be bound never to buy at other shops. The names of the members shall not be made public.

The first step to be taken was to establish our White List. Our Standard of a Fair House had been drafted by the Working Women's Society and modified by us after seeking advice from those firms which had the reputation of treating their employees the most fairly. Fourteen hundred letters were sent to all the retail dry goods and fancy goods shopkeepers in the city, as listed in the directory, with copies of the following:

STANDARD OF A FAIR HOUSE

Wages

A fair house is one in which equal pay is given for work of equal value, irrespective of sex. In the departments where women only are employed, in which the minimum wages are six dollars per week for experienced adult workers, and fall in few instances below eight dollars;

In which wages are paid by the week;

In which fines, if imposed, are paid into a fund for the benefit of the employees;

In which the minimum wages of cash girls are two dollars per week, with the same conditions regarding weekly payments and fines.

Hours

A fair house is one in which the hours from 8 A.M. to 6 P.M. (with three quarters of an hour for lunch) constitute the working day, and a general half-holiday is given on one day of each week during at least two summer months;

In which a vacation of not less than one week is given with pay during the summer season;

In which all overtime is compensated for.

Physical Conditions

A fair house is one in which work, lunch, and retiring rooms are apart from each other, and conform in all respects to the present sanitary laws;

In which the present law regarding the providing of seats for saleswomen is observed, and the use of seats permitted.

Other Conditions

A fair house is one in which humane and considerate behaviour toward employees is the rule;

In which fidelity and length of service meet with the consideration which is their due;

In which no children under fourteen years of age are employed.

Letters were sent to shopkeepers asking them to sign an enclosed agreement as follows:

AGREEMENT TO BE SIGNED BY HEAD OF RETAIL MERCANTILE HOUSE

I, the undersigned, hereby express my desire to conduct my business upon the principles laid down in the Standard of a Fair House, as adopted by the Consumers' League.

I further agree to allow a committee appointed by the Consumers League to visit any part of my business premises and question my employees, and I agree to answer to said committee inquiries as to the following points (the Consumers' League pledging itself that such information shall not be published in detail): Rate of Wages, Holidays, Overtime, Fines, Hours Worked, Meal Times, Sanitary Conditions.

The recipients of the letters were informed that if they felt unable to sign the agreement in its present form, the League would be glad to have them modify it until it met with their approval, and then return it signed.

Thirty papers, out of fourteen hundred, were signed and returned to the secretary of the League. Members of the Governing Board at once visited all the stores represented by these signatures, but they were amazed to find, after investigation, that only four of the thirty who responded actually conformed to the League's Standard of a Fair House. In many of the stores most of the conditions were favourable, but one or two unfavourable ones prevented their being included in the White List.

The principal bugbear seemed to be the non-recognition that overtime existed. Merchants claimed that employees were engaged to work until 10 P.M. on Saturdays, and until the same hour for two to three weeks during the holiday season. These hours, the employers claimed, were taken into consideration when the Wage scale was fixed. The merchants admitted that it was often eleven o'clock or later before customers could be coerced to leave the store, but they saw no necessity to increase wages on that account. Finally, after many consultations and investigations, we published our first White List; it had but eight names:

Aitken, Son & Co., Broadway and Eighteenth Street.
B. Altman & Co., Sixth Avenue and Nineteenth Street.
Arnold, Constable & Co., Broadway and Nineteenth Street.
Lord & Taylor, Broadway and Twentieth Street.
James McCreery & Co., Broadway and Eleventh Street.
E. A. Morrison & Son, Broadway and Nineteenth Street.

The other two stores, to the best of my recollection, were:

The New York Exchange for Women's Work, 329 Fifth Avenue.
The Society of Decorative Art, 28 East Twenty-first Street.

Unfortunately, the record of that first White List seems to have been lost. The second list, published in 1892, contained eleven additional names, as follows:

Best & Co., 60 West Twenty-third Street.
Denning & Co., Broadway and Tenth Street.
Mme. N. G. Felicie, 361 Fifth Avenue.
Harlem Exchange for Women's Work, 40 West One Hundred and Twenty-fifth Street.
L. P. Hollander & Co., 290 Fifth Avenue.
Japanese Trading Co., 18 East Eighteenth Street.
Geo. F. Langenbacher, 820 Broadway.

LeBoutillier Bros., 50 West Twenty-third Street.
Madison Avenue Depository and Exchange for Women's Work, 628 Madison Avenue.
P. A. O. Schwartz, 42 East Fourteenth Street.
A. A. Vantine & Co., 879 Broadway.

This White List was distributed by circulating it in pamphlet form among the members, and also by paying to have it appear as an advertisement in the leading newspapers. What was the reaction of the shopping public and of the merchants? Many of our members who had accounts with firms whose names did not appear on the list visited them and expressed themselves as unwilling to patronize any stores not on the White List of the Consumers' League. But the White List meant little to the general public as yet. The large army of shoppers were unaffected; they continued to hunt their bargains in the same irresponsible manner. If they noticed our advertisements, it meant nothing to them. The reaction, however, of the merchants, was sharp and quick. They did notice our advertisement and resented it. They treated the matter lightly at first; they pooh-poohed the absurd attempts of a handful of "busybodies" who were trying to revolutionize business methods. It never could be done; merchants who gave their entire time and thought to their business knew better how to conduct that business than sentimental, visionary women who had no business training, and who allowed their hearts to run away with their heads. The Consumers' League, they contended, could not survive a year. Women would continue to buy where they found bargains or novelties; they would not be interested in the wages or working conditions of the store employees. Besides, what would housekeepers think if a band of men went about asking questions as to how many hours their housemaids worked, or how late at night they were obliged to continue their service, or whether they were given vacations with pay? Would housekeepers care to answer inquiries as to what kind of food they gave their servants, or what kind of beds they furnished?

These specious arguments cooled the ardour of many members of the Consumers' League. They were not so eager to have an investigation conducted of conditions for household domestics. No better answer to this course of reasoning could be found than the following:[1]

The fallacy is in placing a household in the same category as an industrial enterprise. The function of the industrial business is the creation of wealth; the function of the household is the fulfilment of personal satisfactions, the creation, if possible, of happiness. The business makes money; the household spends it. Labour in a household is personal service; work in a business is industrial investment. Recompense for the first is a fixed stipend calculated upon the income of the person benefited and served; recompense for the second consists in a share in the profits which the work secures—is therefore not fixed, and should not be, but varies with the success of the business.

This is not a sentimental, but an economic classification; it is that of the census, which ranks in one class the professions and domestic servants; physicians, lawyers, clergymen, architects, soldiers, teachers, with manicures, nurses, coachmen, gardeners, cooks. The common bond of union between the different members

[1]From the address of Dr. Mary Putnam Jacobi, given at the annual meeting of the Consumers' League of New York, 1895.

of this class which seems so heterogeneous is the fact that the work in each case is directed toward the personal welfare of some individual who is relatively helpless and often unable to test or estimate the intrinsic value of the service; that is, to know whether it is well done or not, or at all events, how it should be done; and further, that the pecuniary reward of such work can rarely be much more than the living expenses of the worker—cannot, unless invested in strictly industrial enterprises, procure wealth. Hence, as a substitute for wealth, the special rewards of personal service are personal affection, appreciation of fidelity, trust, social honour.

Every detail of this situation is in contrast with that of the industrial enterprise. Almost at the outset of the growth of this the element of personal contact disappears, and at the maximum of expansion, in huge conglomerations of factory labour, personalities themselves are swamped. The servant, whether domestic or professional, contributes nothing to the income of the person he serves and out of which he is paid. The employee is constantly helping to create the fund which is partly returned to him in wages.

Despite the opposition, the specious arguments, the indignation of the merchants; despite the indifference, the irresponsibility, the carelessness of the general shopping public, we did survive our first year. By the end of the second year, 1893, we were able to publish a White List of twenty-four names, three times as many as appeared in the original list.

The courage and determination of one frail woman of humble origin had succeeded in raising the standard of industrial conditions for thousands of working girls.

CHAPTER III

DEVELOPMENT OF THE IDEA

It is not enough to know, we must also apply;
It is not enough to will, we must also do.
—GOETHE.

To do, to strive, to know, and with the knowing,
To find life's widest purpose in our growing.
—CHARLOTTE PERKINS GILMAN.

HOW did we succeed within the short space of two years in putting twenty-four names on our White List? This story presented many phases of social, educational, and economic problems. In the meeting and solving of them, there were many amusing as well as tragic incidents. Whenever a new name was added to the White List, competitive jealousy was aroused. The merchants whose stores were omitted from the White List scoffed and jeered at it and asked their inquisitive customers in what way their conditions differed from their neighbours' conditions. The customers were not always able to answer these questions, but passed them on to the Consumers' League. Then details and specific facts were reported by those who had investigated, and the result usually was that members of firms not on the White List would finally send to the League for a committee to call to talk matters over. Amicable discussions would ensue. The great impasse seemed to be the mooted question as to whether 6 P. M. should be considered the legitimate close of the working day. The firms that catered to a fashionable public were not obliged to keep their stores open of an evening; their customers never shopped after daylight hours. However, it did not seem fair to those merchants who catered also to working men and women, and who were forced to a realization of the fact that these customers were not free until evening, that they should be debarred from the White List because they felt obliged to have longer hours. We appreciated this distinction and sought to coöperate with the merchants by agreeing to educate the shopping public to shop earlier in the day if the merchants would agree to give "time off" to saleswomen during the early hours of the morning, in return for the extra time demanded of an evening.

This concession was made by several firms, the extra time being given in lieu of extra pay. We considered this a great triumph, as it marked the recognition of the fact that for stores, as well as for factories, 6 P. M. was the legitimate closing hour. In those days the working day began at 8 A. M., ten hours being considered a working day. Those firms which kept open of an evening for ten days to two weeks during the holiday season were asked to give "time off," later on, for as many extra hours as the saleswomen had worked during that period. The opening wedge in giving wage compensation for overtime work came when a certain firm, owning a large department store, gave to the saleswomen a percentage of the sales made during the

Christmas holiday season. A newspaper article, commenting on this interesting experiment, mentioned that it not only served to stimulate sales, but improved the quality of the service by causing the employees to be more attentive and polite to customers. It was stated that this feature was so marked that it was frequently commented upon by patrons of the establishment.

In 1895 the Consumers' League made an interesting computation of the number of hours of unpaid work given by the employees to their employers, in sixteen of the largest dry goods houses in New York City. By multiplying the number of employees of each firm by the number of days at the holiday season, during which the stores were kept open of an evening (testified to by their own advertisements), and this number again multiplied by four (the number of hours from 6 to 10 P. M.) the result was amazing. It showed that in the aggregate these sixteen firms exacted, during the one holiday season, 600,200 hours of free labour, or 60,020 working days of ten hours each, which by actual calculation amounted to 191 years and some months. This was the Christmas present made by the employees to their employers! The cost of this gift to those who gave it may be judged by the following excerpt from an issue of *St. George's Chronicle*, published in 1895 and signed by the rector of St. George's Church, Rev. W. S. Rainsford:

A BLACK LIST

On Christmas Day, when in the homes of many of us life is at its brightest, it seems unnatural and almost wrong to indulge in careful or sorrowful thoughts. Yet, if we would obey Him who has brought Christmas and all it means into our lives, we must be careful to look on the things of others as well as our own things. Many such there are who need our help. Life cannot be made tolerable or sweet without that help. I know of scores in our own church, who, through no fault of their own, but by the harsh circumstances and drudgery of their lives, must find Christmas a mockery. Let me only, by way of example, mention two or three of these that I know:

Lily B—— works at M——'s. For the ten days before Christmas she worked till 10:30 P. M. every week night, and from nine in the morning till five on Sunday. No food was provided while the young girl endured this strain. She gets four dollars a week as regular wages. When she got home on Christmas Eve she fainted from exhaustion.

Lillie L——, at L——'s. Kept until eleven o'clock several days before Christmas. On Christmas Eve kept until 12:30 midnight. Nothing to eat. No extra pay. Wages, three dollars a week.

These are young girls. Such work as this simply destroys their youth and prepares them, aye, and many thousands like them, for a faulty and decrepit womanhood. What are we going to do about it? We should not deal at these stores.

This closing sentence of Doctor Rainsford's is an indication of how our propaganda was beginning to find its way into the consciousness of groups of people who were naturally conscientious, but had not yet awakened to the fact that the Hebrew word *Tsedakah* stood for justice as well as for charity. One of the firms mentioned in *St. George's Chronicle* is no longer in business; the other firm secured a place on our White List eight years later.

One of the reactions from some of the merchants con-stituted a very interesting phase of the development; it will serve as a good illustration of the fairness and justice of the League's attitude toward both merchant

and public. Some firms were so scornful of our White
List that they refused to permit any investigations,
even where their standards would have warranted
their names being placed on the list. Mrs. Lowell
had such a keen sense of justice that, after having gained
the required information through the Working Women's
Society and through the firms' employees, these stores
were placed on the White List without the firms'
consent or approval. It is interesting to note that,
once included, these firms never asked us to remove
their names.

The Governing Board of the Consumers' League
asked its members to hold parlour meetings in their
homes, in order to enlist the interest of their friends.
Meetings were also arranged to be held at church
guilds and neighbourhood settlements. Speakers were
also sent to address groups of women at their club
meetings. In this way, an ever-increasing membership
was obtained. It was always pointed out at these
meetings that the responsibility for existing evils in
industrial conditions lay, in a large measure, upon
the shoulders of the consumers. If hours were long
in stores, it was due primarily to the fact that the
shoppers shopped at a late hour; if stores were kept open
late during the holiday season, it was because shoppers
left the purchase of their Christmas gifts until the last
moment, and instead of shopping early in the season
and early in the day, they were adding to the pressure
of exhausting days prolonged far into the night. We
showed that if shoppers did not pay their bills when
presented, they were often the means of preventing

employees from getting their wages paid promptly. This was true of small stores, where the employer depended upon the cash received from sales for the payment of weekly wages. We asked for fair treatment of merchants as well as for fair treatment for working girls. We tried to raise the standard of ethics in money-spending as well as in money-making. We pointed out that merchants were forced to include in the price fixed on goods the cost of delivery and the cost of sending for them to be credited when returned. This custom of sending home hats, garments, and all kinds of articles which were constantly returned to be credited within a few days was an abuse of a privilege indulged in by many shoppers with apparently no conscience at all. It was known that prominent wealthy women would have handsome opera cloaks sent home "on approval," and after wearing them, would return them to be credited the following day. Indeed, on one such occasion an initialled handkerchief was found in the pocket by the saleswoman when it was returned. We asked shoppers to shorten the working day of delivery clerks by refusing to receive packages after six o'clock at night. We asked them to specify when making purchases that packages could be sent the following day; when there was immediate need of the article, it could be taken by the purchaser or else purchased early in the day. We showed that carelessness in giving addresses for packages to be sent often resulted in real hardship to saleswomen. For if clerks took down wrong addresses and packages were lost, the clerks were blamed and were fined for the first offence and apt to be dismissed the second time it occurred. Then we showed how much power to remedy conditions consumers really had. We related how the wife of one of the ex-Governors of New York State was passing a counter in one of the high-class department stores, and happened to see one of the saleswomen faint. She followed her to the retiring room in the basement, where she was laid on the concrete floor. After she recovered, the ex-Governor's wife took her home in her carriage. She learned that she had been nursing a sick mother and had had little or no sleep the previous night.

"But why didn't you sit down," the lady asked, "since there were no customers to be waited upon?"

"There are no seats provided," the girl responded, "and besides, one of the rules of the store is 'No sitting down on boxes or on ledge at back of counter, and no leaning against each other!'"

The kind-hearted lady was horrified. The next day she paid a visit to the private office of the head of the firm. Her ultimatum was: "Seats behind counters for salesgirls or I withdraw my account!"

Her account was sufficiently important to seem desirable of retention. The following day a consignment of three-legged stools, such as are used by milkmaids, were distributed behind those counters which were presided over by the weaker sex. They were not wasted on salesmen, who were considered sufficiently strong physically to be immune from weariness. A legend relates that when the girls saw the stools, they *all* fainted, one after another!

It is one thing to provide stools and another thing to permit the use of them. It did not take long for investigators of the Consumers' League to discover that sometimes, where plenty of seats were provided, it was an unwritten law that whosoever used them was dismissed, or at least reprimanded. It was found that in many instances it was the floor-walker of the department in question who was the strict disciplinarian, and that the members of the firm were oblivious of the fact. The League found, upon investigating, that there was a city ordinance providing for seats behind counters, but as it had been so loosely drawn and there were no inspectors to enforce it, it was a dead letter.

The story of the fainting girl stretched out on the concrete floor awakened the League to the necessity of rest rooms as well as seats behind counters. The need of this innovation was brought to the attention of merchants. How did the merchants respond to our request? The majority scoffed at the idea. A few of them were wise enough to realize that a short, needed rest might enable the worker to finish her day's work, whereas without it, the firm might lose a half day's service.

This might be considered as a nucleus of the idea that efficiency could be increased through good working conditions. These first rest rooms could hardly be deserving of the term, yet they were a step forward. For instance, in a certain department store the rest room was far from being what its name denoted. It was in the sub-basement, where it was so dark that flickering gas jets were necessary; it was partitioned

off from the packing department, where the sound of
hammering of heavy boxes and dragging them about
was heard all day. There was no fresh air or proper
ventilation. A strap and pulley from some machinery
was winding itself noisily above the cot which had been
placed in the partition for any employee who suddenly
felt ill. An appeal had been made to one member
of the firm to provide a better space for the rest room,
but he contended that there was no other place available. So we sought some ruse to bring about the desired end. I invited this merchant's wife to take a
drive with me one day, and during the course of the
conversation I asked whether she had ever seen the
"rest room" in question. She had not; she never
interfered in her husband's business. She felt that he
knew best how to conduct it. A description of the
room and a suggestion as to women understanding
these particular matters better than men, sufficed to
arouse her interest. Not long afterwards the rest room
was moved to another part of the building and was
fitted up with a cabinet containing all that was needed
for first aid to the injured.

Our campaign against delayed Christmas shopping
forms an interesting story in itself. It seems almost
impossible to-day to realize how difficult it was at first
to arouse public interest. We were told that the
crowded stores just before the holiday and the brilliant
illumination of them at night added to the Christmas
spirit and portrayed cheer and good fellowship.
Besides, how could shoppers make a selection of gifts
when articles were not displayed until a few weeks

before the holiday and attractive, marked-down sales occurred only a few days before? We addressed groups of women at their club meetings, at their church guild meetings; we told them some of the stories which had come to our notice of salesgirls and cash-girls who had broken down under the strain. Our listeners were made to realize the evil effect of extreme fatigue and exhaustion. We told of girls who were obliged to go to hospitals immediately after the holidays, in order to regain their strength and health. It often required months for them to recover so that they felt their old-time vigour. We endeavoured to secure the coöperation of merchants by asking them to display their Christmas gifts earlier in the season. We found that just as soon as the demand for these gifts was made, the supply was forthcoming.

We succeeded in getting one of the largest department firms to place a leaflet in every package delivered during the first weeks of December. This leaflet set forth the necessity for shopping early in the season and early in the day. In a few concise statements appropriate to this admonition, it gave briefly the aims and principles of the Consumers' League. The *Survey* magazine coöperated in endeavouring to extend the early Christmas shopping movement throughout the country. Later on, several storekeepers aided in spreading the propaganda by placing cards in packages delivered during December.

Another interesting feature of the League's propaganda was the urging of educators and of the clergy to hold a "Consumers' League Week-End" just after

Thanksgiving. We asked the principals of the schools to direct the attention of their pupils to the necessity of early Christmas shopping, and we gave leaflets to be distributed. We asked the clergymen to give this subject consideration in their sermon of that week. From the pulpits of the churches and the synagogues went forth the plea for the observance of Consumers' League principles. In some of the church vestibules our leaflets were distributed.

At last we created so much interest in the movement that we were able to hang a huge banner across Twenty-third Street, then the centre of the shopping district, reminding women to do their Christmas shopping early. We secured permission from the city authorities, and we also had the good will of two firms on opposite sides of the street, who permitted us to use their windows for attaching the ends of the rope from which the banner was suspended. This was the first time any banner, not used for political purposes, was seen to stream conspicuously above the populace in New York City. It made quite a sensation, and gathered crowds of people, some of whom learned for the first time that a consumers' league existed and had its headquarters at the United Charities Building, 105 East twenty-second Street. This knowledge spread among the working girls, and from that time we had many communications from them, some of them signed, and some sent anonymously. One young woman to whom an inquiry was addressed across the counter said: "Oh, yes, now we have seats and the floor-walker sees us sitting on them and doesn't tell us to get up. And we are no longer told to hurry our luncheon and return to the counter in ten minutes, as we used to be told. There is a bunch of society women working for us now, and they'll never know the amount of good they've done!" This was a tribute which was encouraging to the members of the League. For our work was never completed. Our White Lists had to be gone over every year; we were obliged to visit each store on the list at least once a year, in order to ascertain whether standards were maintained; at that time, there was no law authorizing legal inspectors for retail establishments, although the Working Women's Society had been trying for some years to get such a bill passed. The Consumers' League, therefore, constituted itself a body of volunteer inspectors. We considered ourselves *official*, the merchants termed us *officious;* nevertheless, they were compelled to recognize the force of public opinion.

Sometimes it happened that a firm which had made an effort to reach our standard, in order to be included in the White List, would slip back after having attained the desired goal. When this was brought to our attention, if our pleadings for genuine reformation were unsuccessful, we were obliged to drop the delinquent firm from our list. This did not happen frequently, as it gave to the Board that crushing sense of failure which a mother feels when her erring child strays from the path of virtue and fails to uphold the standards she had taught him. And again, when, like the prodigal son, such a firm mended its ways and returned to the fold, there was much rejoicing among the members of the Board.

The printing of all these White Lists constituted a great expense, especially as black-listing was illegal, and therefore we were not allowed by law to draw a line through a name already on our list. So, if we were compelled to drop a firm, we were obliged to destroy all the old lists and print new ones, leaving out the delinquent firm. With all this expense, we found we could no longer depend upon voluntary contributions; we decided to tax our members $1 a year. Up to this time there had been no annual dues; attaching a signature to our principles and aims had constituted membership. The reaction to this innovation would have been amusing had it not seemed so tragic to us. Our long membership list, of which we had been so proud, shrank visibly and rapidly. Some of the members who had been most importunate about receiving large quantities of pamphlets for distribution resigned when they found they could no longer get them without a small fee; others gave as excuse their projected absence from town; a few preferred to die! However, although the membership list was smaller, those who remained with us were earnest, faithful workers, with a strong sense of responsibility, and as the new membership list grew it was women of this calibre who followed our banner.

Another great expense was the advertising of our White List in the newspapers. As the list grew and as we required more space, the expense mounted.

Then arose another interesting development in regard to the advertising of this White List. Whereas at first the merchants were disdainful of it, it was not long be- fore they came to feel the force and power that lay behind that small, apparently insignificant advertise- ment. Firms which advertised in the daily papers whose names did not appear on the list, objected to its publication and threatened to withdraw their daily costly advertisements if the editors continued to insert our modest notice. One newspaper editor after another felt it was necessary to refuse our advertisement; they could not afford to let their advertising business go to their rival papers. The editors of one paper only, the New York *Evening Post*, stood out against the pressure brought to bear, and I am glad of this opportunity to pay my tribute to their courage. A well-known firm owning a large department store withdrew its full-page advertisement for one year, thus causing the editors a large financial loss. During this time our small notice appeared with regularity. It was a matter of high principle with the editors of the *Post;* they maintained that their large advertisers could not con- trol their policy. The Consumers' League came to realize that these principles were being upheld at too great a sacrifice on the part of the editors, so we with- drew our advertisement. This did not mean that we ceased to publish the White List. Our Board had indomitable will, plenty of originality and initiative, and we soon found other methods of getting our propa- ganda before the public. We advertised in theatre programmes, in omnibuses, in subway and elevated trains. We had White Lists framed and placed in waiting rooms of hotels, and we were permitted to place them in a few of the White List stores. The members of the League distributed them widely when travelling.

Perhaps no better example could be given of the development of the public conscience and the growth of public opinion than the story of how we finally obtained the necessary legislation to improve the working conditions of women and children in New York State. For five years we had been supporting the Working Women's Society in its effort to get legislation enacted at Albany which would bring about better working conditions in the stores. Each year, the bill which had been carefully drafted failed of passage. Finally, it passed the Assembly, and in the Senate was referred to the Rhinehart Commission—a committee which had recently been appointed "to investigate the conditions of work for female labour in New York State," with Senator Rhinehart as chairman of the Commission. Indeed, this Commission had been appointed because knowledge of working conditions had been brought to the attention of Senators through the investigations of the Consumers' League. Therefore, the Commission naturally turned to us for help in their investigations. They called upon us for a large share of testimony which our officers and directors gladly gave. This testimony in regard to existing conditions found in stores, workrooms, and sweatshops, was all given under oath. The following are a few extracts from the report of the Commission:

WAGES

There is no doubt that low wages prevail in these establishments, and that the wages are not as an average adequate compensation for the work done or the hours of labour employed.

HOURS

After stating that numerous houses are open only from 8 A.M. to 6 P.M. six days each week, the report proceeds:

Other places keep their employees at work the same number of hours on all days except Saturdays, and on Saturdays keep their stores open until 8, 9, and even 12 o'clock at night. Others were found which kept open every night until 9, 10, or 11 o'clock, and on Sundays from two to four hours. . . . After a full consideration, the Committee is of the opinion that the limitation of ten hours a day applicable to other days in the week should not be extended to Saturday. The employee, even though Saturday is excepted, will not be compelled to work more than sixty hours a week; while the employer, if he desires to have the labour of the employees on Saturday night any number of hours over ten hours for that day, must arrange the employment of his employees so that the excess number of hours of labour on Saturday shall be deducted from the number of hours of labour on some other day or days of the week. This provision can entail no hardship upon either the employer or the employees, because the distribution of the hours of labour throughout the week can be readily and easily arranged. In calculating the hours of labour, the lunch time should be included and credited to the employee.

SEATS

The Committee is satisfied from personal investigation that this law (Chapter 298, Laws of 1881) has been constantly evaded, and that in many retail establishments suitable seats are not maintained, and that the female employees have not the right to use such seats at reasonable times. The importance of providing proper seats and of permitting their use at reasonable times cannot be overestimated.

The Committee, from the testimony had before it, and the personal visits made to mercantile establishments, is of the opinion that the proper proportion should be one seat to every three female employees, and these seats should be placed where it is possible and convenient for the employees to use them, that is to say, behind the counters, tables, or desks where the women work. In order to guard against evasions of the law, a seat . . . should be permanent in character, that is to say, attached to the floor or counter, or wall, or shelving, so that employers may not, as many of them have done in the past, provide movable wooden and paper boxes and contend that they are "suitable seats." _ . . .

BASEMENTS

It appeared from the testimony of some of the employees, and from personal visits of the Committee, that some of the basements of the retail mercantile stores were not properly lighted or ventilated, and that work therein was injurious to the health of the employees. Practically all of these basements are lighted by artificial light, and ventilated by artificial means of ventilation, and women, girls, and boys work for ten hours a day with only an intermission for lunch time, without seeing the sunlight, in places ventilated by fans or other contrivances. . . .

CONCLUSION OF REPORT

The contention was repeatedly made before the Committee that many of the mercantile houses were being carried on in the same manner as if there was a law forcing them to comply with the above specific provisions, and that those mercantile establishments which were not carrying on their business in that way would be forced to do so by the demands of the public and the ordinary laws of competition. The Committee therefore arrived at the conclusion that those employers who are now carrying on their business the same as they would if there were a law, instead of being affected disadvantageously by such a law, would be benefited, by reason of the fact that all other establishments would be required to conform with the standards established by such a law; and as to those employers who are not conducting their business places as it is intended they should under the proposed law, the Committee believes that such a law is necessary and indeed imperative in the interests of the public welfare.

As a result of these findings the Mercantile Inspection Act was passed in the spring of 1896 and went into effect the following September. It applied to towns of more than 3,000 inhabitants, to all places where goods were sold. It contained many of the provisions for which the Consumers' League had been working six years to procure. It embodied, briefly:

A sixty-hour-a-week clause for young women under twenty-one and boys under sixteen, and provided for a working day of ten hours, not to begin before 7 A. M. or to last after 10 P. M. (Unfortunately this provision did not apply to the holiday season from December 15th to January 1st.) It prohibited employment of children under fourteen and demanded for children under sixteen a certificate of age, health, and school attendance. The bill also demanded proper sanitary arrangements regarding retiring rooms, lunch rooms, and basements, and also required the placement of one seat behind counters for every three saleswomen. The enforcement of the bill was placed under the supervision of the local Boards of Health. Firms were required to post a copy of the bill in three conspicuous places in each establishment.

It was scarcely more than six years since Alice Woodbridge had roused us to action by the reading of her startling report, and this recognition of the facts she had presented, by the law-making body of our state, was a triumph so great that all the struggle and strain of the past years were forgotten in the inspiration that we found for wider fields. The nature of the insidious obstacles which we had to overcome in order to arouse the public to a realization of facts can be exemplified by what took place when we gave our testimony before the Rhinehart Commission.

It was very noticeable that the newspapers, when reviewing the testimony which created quite a sensation at the time, only printed the names of firms which were not large advertisers, whereas the firms which had full-page or half-page advertisements were singularly protected from the prying eyes of a too curious shopping public. The portion of testimony referring to them was either totally excluded from their columns, or else the name of the firm was omitted. For instance, on one occasion I gave testimony as to the lack of seats in a well-known store on Fourteenth Street; I related an account of the conversation held with a member of the firm and repeated his picturesque and profane language in refusing to install seats for saleswomen. A reporter told me that it would make the best "story" of any testimony given during that day, but it would be impossible to get it into the papers, as the firm in question was among the largest advertisers. As a matter of fact, all mention of the firm's conditions was suppressed. However, a full report of the testimony given in regard to an insignificant neighbourhood store on upper Columbus Avenue was printed with the name and address of the firm, since, obviously, *they* had never advertised. This proprietor's reply, when asked whether he would be willing to place seats behind counters and permit saleswomen to use them when not engaged in waiting on customers was characteristic of the sentiment expressed by most employers at that time: "My store is not a hospital," he said. "I would dismiss any clerk who dared to sit down during working hours. I pay them to *stand* behind counters and sell goods." When this appeared in cold print the following morning, it seemed heartless and unsympathetic even to the proprietor himself. He wrote letters denying that he had ever made such a statement, and he threatened to sue me for having testified falsely. This letter was handed to Senator Rhinehart who, after reading it, announced that witnesses would be protected by the state and that they need not be alarmed by any threats of damage suits because of giving testimony. I never heard any further from the store proprietor in question. These facts prove that advertisers—statements of editors notwithstanding—*did* control to a very large extent the news columns of our daily papers, as I have previously asserted.

In drafting the Mercantile Bill we had asked to have the responsibility for the supervision of stores and the enforcement of the law placed upon the state factory inspector. Instead of this, the local Departments of Health were given the supervision and enforcement of the new law. It was explained that it would increase the State Tax Budget too much to increase the force of state factory inspectors required for the additional supervision of stores, so the directors of the Consumers' League, fearing that the bill would not be passed at all if they did not yield this point, yielded, and the bill was passed.

When the new law went into operation the sanitary inspectors of local Boards of Health were expected to

include retail stores in their inspections, but it soon
developed that this additional work was considered
unimportant compared with larger fields of work, and,
moreover, the inspectors claimed that this new duty
overloaded their department. We found that although
we had finally succeeded in getting the law placed
on our statute books, it was constantly being evaded
and was most difficult of enforcement; this was largely
due to lack of proper inspection.

In 1902, Dr. Ernst Lederle, the Commissioner of the
Department of Health, appointed me as a special inspector, without salary, and furnished me with the
shield of the department which gave me the official
authority to investigate and question. My findings
were reported to the department. By this time my
position as president of the New York Consumers'
League was so well recognized that several of the merchants resented the power that had been given me,
and made a formal protest to the Commissioner against
my appointment. Doctor Lederle's reply was to the
effect that, if they were obeying the law, they had nothing to fear; if they were violating it, he wished to know
the facts. The New York Consumers' League, realizing the necessity of regular inspection, bent its efforts
toward getting the Board of Estimate and Apportion-
ment to appropriate a specific sum for the purpose of
adding to the corps of inspectors in the Department of
Health. These additional inspectors were to be given
charge of retail stores. We succeeded in getting a few
mercantile inspectors appointed, but the number was inadequate.

After twelve years of this more or less desultory and sporadic supervision by officers of Health Departments, the Mercantile Law was amended so as to place the responsibility for its enforcement where it really belonged, upon the chief factory inspector. In 1908, the Department of Labour was reorganized and the chief factory inspector became known as the State Labour Commissioner. The special work of enforcing the Mercantile Law now devolved upon a chief mercantile inspector with a small staff of inspectors.

The Labour Commissioner was appointed with a view to pleasing the labour leaders, but he had to be a man also who would not antagonize employers. At first, labour leaders were suspicious of the Consumers' League movement, not having much faith in our altruistic motives; they felt that no reforms could be accomplished unless started and carried out by the workers themselves. Later on, however, the wiser ones realized that results warranted their coöperation, and whenever the Consumers' League officers and directors went to Albany to plead for necessary amendments of laws, we were reinforced by one or two speakers from the Federation of Labour.

And now, although I am getting ahead of my story, it seems pertinent to relate the following incident: Governor Altgeld of Illinois had been sufficiently progressive to appoint in 1893 a woman as chief factory inspector—Mrs. Florence Kelley. His choice had been so admirable that she failed to secure a reappointment because she had enforced the factory laws so fairly and impartially that a protest went up from those

manufacturers who did not wish to have the law enforced. There could not have been a finer or more
subtle tribute. In 1899, the National Consumers'
League was organized with headquarters in New York
and Mrs. Kelley was asked to be the general secretary.
Mrs. Kelley's previous experience and the knowledge
she had gained through her work in connection with
the Consumers' League seemed to us to make her
peculiarly well fitted for the post of factory inspector.
The appointment for this post was just then being
canvassed. I went to Albany to interview Governor
Roosevelt, feeling confident that he would see the wisdom of appointing one so well equipped for the post.
But while the Governor was entirely in sympathy with
the aims and ideals of the Consumers' League, and
recognized Mrs. Kelley's ability, he was quite frank in
pointing out to me that the time was not ripe for the
Governor of New York State to appoint a woman as
factory inspector; he said that his constituents would
not stand for it; they were urging him to appoint a certain man and nothing would be gained by opposing their
wishes in this matter. I learned later that the man in
question ran an elevator in the Capitol, at Albany; he
had succeeded in ingratiating himself with the legisla-
tors, and when, through their influence, he secured the
appointment, his ignorance of the duties involved necessitated his going to Boston to learn from the Massachusetts factory inspector what was expected of him.
    As the work of the League became known, working
girls began to send us communications, telling us of
evils which ought to be abolished, of infractions of the

law, of unprincipled floor-walkers who were trying to corrupt young girls. The League always endeavoured to protect the writer of a complaint. We kept the original document on file and copied the complaint on our own stationery, refusing to divulge any facts which would lead to the discovery of the identity of the writer. In one instance, however, notwithstanding our care, the case of a complaint was sifted by the employers who were engaged in the making of *Bibles*. They decided that the complaint had been made by one of three girls; not being sure which was the guilty one, they were considering dismissing all three. Thereupon, the one who had written the letter, not wishing her comrades to suffer on her account, confessed and was promptly discharged. Yet her complaint had been warranted; the firm had not complied with the existing law, and the League had, after investigation, considered that she had been fully justified in writing to us. The directors of the League were fortunate in being able to secure another position for her.

The League frequently found itself in the position of a Court of Arbitration. For instance, an employee in the dressmaking department of one of the leading department stores was strongly advised by her physician to take a vacation; she had an invalid mother whom she was supporting, and she was on the verge of breaking down under the care and responsibility. She feared that if she asked for a vacation she might not be able to hold her position. Her physician and her clergyman, therefore, appealed to her employers to grant her a leave of absence of four weeks and to promise to take her back at the end of that time. They agreed. They told the young woman that they would not engage any one else in her place, and that when she returned she could have the same position again. During her absence two of the other employees in the department worked harder and did as much as had been previously done by three. So the firm decided to pay them a little more and abolish the position of the third. The employee who had taken the vacation gained so rapidly in strength that she returned at the end of three weeks, instead of remaining away the full quota of four weeks allowed her. When she was informed that her position had been abolished, she was staggered. The firm contended that they had not broken their word, because no one else had been taken in her place; they had merely done away with that particular position. The shock and the dread of perhaps not being able to secure a remunerative position elsewhere at once sent her to bed, where she was kept under the doctor's care for some time. The Consumers' League received its information about the case from the girl's clergyman, who was indignant that the firm in question was on the White List of the League. We wrote a letter to the firm, asking for an interview; we received no reply. We decided to call without an appointment. We bearded the lion—the head of the firm—in his *sanctum sanctorum*—his private office, which we were not supposed to enter without first being announced and receiving permission. But we did not stand on ceremony, we swept aside the various watchdogs at the entrance and stalked in, taking the gentleman unawares as he was about to leave to enjoy his luncheon. He was much annoyed at first, telling us that he didn't give a hang whether he was on the White List or not; indeed, he preferred to have his name taken off. The Directors of the League were a group of busy-bodies who poked their noses into people's private business affairs, and they thought they knew better than the business men themselves how to manage their business! But he calmed down after a while and ad-mitted that the firm's code of ethics in dealing with customers was on a higher plane than when concerned with the employees. He admitted that the employee in question had not had a square deal and he handed us a check of $40 to pay for her vacation. He even expressed a willingness to take her back, but we had already placed her with one of his competitors, and she was getting a slight advance in wages. As we were leaving his office an hour or more beyond the luncheon hour, he snatched up his hat, and remarked that he hoped we were not as hungry as he was. Then, with a twinkle in his eye, he said, "And mind, don't you take me off the White List, and don't report this incident in your year book!" We handed the check to the vic-tim of the "misunderstanding," and we were sufficiently magnanimous to refrain from boasting of our achieve-ment in behalf of the down-trodden working girl, one of many who would have frequently been exploited had the League not come to the rescue.

These stories serve to illustrate the Consumers' League's attitude in its effort to prevent the exploita-tion of the helpless working girl unprotected by legislation. However, it cannot be too strongly emphasized that we never sentimentally put the rights of the employee above the rights of the employer. We recognized that, while he must act justly and fairly to his employees, they owed him a very positive duty, and this duty we tried on all occasions to uphold by addressing groups of working girls. We drew their attention to industrial laws and the penalties for violation, but we emphasized the necessity of their giving faithful service in return for a fair remuneration and just conditions.

I cannot dwell too strongly upon the fact that the work of the Consumers' League lay along the lines of true economics. Although our sympathies may have been aroused, we were not guided by a false sentiment; we tried to adjust fairly the differences between employer and employee, through the power of the third factor, the consumer.

The passage of the Mercantile Bill in Albany in 1896 and the proper enforcing of the laws marked an era for the Consumers' League. Before that, our work had been formative, in a 'sense, experimental. We had succeeded in arousing the public conscience as to the existence of certain evils and the sense of responsibility for these evils. We had created a public opinion which finally crystallized in legislation. We were no longer a doubtful experiment; we were a force and a power, and we had to be reckoned with.

CHAPTER IV

No one of us can make the world move on very far, but it moves *at all* only when each one of a very large number does his duty.

—THEODORE ROOSEVELT.

D URING the first five years of our work we were so absorbed endeavouring to better local conditions that we did not realize that the news of the movement was spreading rapidly to other cities. In the year 1896, Mrs. Lowell having resigned as president, I was elected to fill the vacancy. About this time requests began to come from Brooklyn, Philadelphia, Boston, and other cities for help in organizing similar leagues to ours. It was considered my duty as president of the parent league (the New York City League), to assist in the creation of these new groups, and these proved to be the nucleus of what was destined to become a national movement. Brooklyn and Philadelphia were the first two leagues to be organized outside of New York City. It is interesting to recall the character of the people who started the movement in the various communities. In Brooklyn, Mrs. Sessions, sister of Rev. Dr. Huntington, of Grace Church, New York, was the organizer and first president. In Philadelphia, the initial meeting at which I was invited to speak was held under the auspices of the Ethical Culture Society of which Mr. William Saltus was the leader. In Boston, many of the professors of Harvard University, of Wellesley College, and members of the Massachusetts Federation of Women's Clubs crowded the large Y. M. C. A. hall on Boylston Street at a meeting which was presided over by Dr. John Graham Brooks, who afterwards became the first president of the National Consumers' League. When, later, Doctor Brooks gave a course of lectures in Chicago on Industrial Conditions, a group of women, some of whom had been doing social service work at Hull House, formed the Illinois League. In the meantime, our local activities did not lessen, they increased. In 1898, there was trouble in the ladies' tailoring industry in New York City. The heads of the industry called it a strike. The employees called it a lockout, and the workers appealed to the Consumers' League to investigate and to help them in their difficulties. We found that nearly all the fashionable ladies' tailors, while they provided elaborate showrooms and fitting rooms for their customers, gave many of their garments to be made up in the tenement homes of the workers. If women pay high prices for clothes, it would seem proper to ask as an equivalent, not only stylish and well-fitting tailored suits, but suits made in regularly inspected sanitary workrooms and not in the living rooms of the workers.

It is claimed that the original cause of the agitation in England, that led to the passage of the Act requiring the making of government goods in factories, was the sad death of the daughter of Sir Robert Peel, twice Prime Minister of England. It was learned, upon investigation, that she had been stricken with typhus fever, as a result of wearing a germ-infected riding habit, which, although ordered and fitted at a fashionable and expensive Regent Street tailor's, had been made in the tenement rooms of the worker. This poverty-stricken workman had two children suffering from this contagious disease, and when he saw them shivering from the cold, he had thrown the skirt of the habit over the bed as an extra protection.[1]

Upon looking into the merits of the controversy that was going on between the New York ladies' tailoring establishments and their employees, we found conditions existed that were similar in character to those that had existed in England prior to the passage of the Act referred to. No doubt, unknown tragedies had occurred from the same cause in our own midst. It was our duty to acquaint the public with the result of our investigation, and to create a sentiment against the buying of wearing apparel made by underpaid workers, under unsanitary conditions. We found that there was a law on the statute books prohibiting the manufacture of clothing in the living rooms of the workers, except when made by the immediate members of the family living in the rooms. This law was constantly evaded, and the factory inspectors were forced to devote a great deal of their time to seeking out and exposing such evasions. The sympathies of the Consumers' League were not always with strikers; on other occasions, we had thrown the weight of our influence with employers, but in this instance we felt that the workers employed had a real grievance. The health

---

[1]From the report of the president of the Consumers' League of the City of New York, 1898.

and welfare of the community demanded that this grievance be remedied. For this grievance was like a two-edged sword: it cut deep into the lives of the consumer as well as of the worker. As workers could not afford a rental sufficient to cover separate workrooms, the work had to be done in bedrooms and kitchens; the tools of the trade, machines, needles, thread, scissors, had to be supplied by the workers themselves; the irons, too, as well as the fuel to heat them; in the dark afternoons of winter the extra gas used was added to their expense. In calling for and returning the work, the workers lost, not only much valuable time, but also had the additional expense of carfare. In the elegant fitting rooms of a high-grade ladies' tailoring establishment, the proprietor would superintend the fittings, but the little unknown tailor from the tenement hovel had to be present, if not to do the actual fitting, at least to see what alterations were required. When a customer was late or broke an appointment, little did she realize the hardship that her carelessness inflicted upon the little unknown tailor. He had to pay double carfare and lose double time. Through the working of this sweatshop system, the proprietor of the establishment saved the rental of workrooms and their equipment, he saved on fuel and on light, and also paid a lower wage than he would have done had the workers been employed to work under his own roof. It was a system that entailed hardship on the worker and was a direct menace to the health of the community. Our sympathies were aroused to such an extent that some of the officers of the League turned their parlours into

fitting rooms. They asked their friends to place orders
with the locked-out workmen, so as to provide them
with the wherewithal necessary to support their families. The newspapers made a great deal of this incident, which advertised us to such a degree that many
women came to our office to ask where they could have
their tailored suits made without having the goods
sent into tenement homes. This demand resulted in
our compiling a White List of ladies' tailors. This
list was never published because of the impossibility of
investigating every such establishment in the city; in all
fairness this would have been necessary before such
publication. What we did was to investigate every
firm whose name was brought to us by customers seeking information. If a customer found that her tailor
gave out his goods to be made up in tenement rooms,
she either forced him to change his methods or she gave
up her custom. The list thus compiled was kept on
file at our office and was shown at the request of any
one who desired to have her suits made on the premises
of the tailor.

As a result of the attitude of the Consumers' League
toward the situation which was brought to light
through the strike, and to the publicity given to the
matter, many of the leading ladies' tailors changed
their methods. Some of them moved into larger quarters, in order to have commodious, well-lighted workrooms. A few advertised that all their work, including
embroidery, was done on the premises. Again the power
wielded by the consumer was felt in the community.

We found that the ladies' tailoring trade was not the

only one that was underpaid and in which conditions were a menace to the public health. Nor did we find, as had often been claimed, that it was women's demand for bargains that forced manufacturers to underpay workers. The League found that, in many instances, consumers paid high prices for goods, yet the actual producers received but a very small percentage of the amount. For example: for hemstitching fine batiste collars which sold for $1 apiece retail, workers received from the retail merchants 25 cents per dozen for the work. The price paid for making boys' reefers with broad sailor collars trimmed with braid was 25 cents per dozen; for making girls' aprons with ruffles and sashes trimmed with edging and sometimes with insertion, 25 cents to 45 cents per dozen; for making nightgowns with embroidery and tucked yokes—thread furnished and embroidery cut out by the workers—$1 a dozen; silk waists 98 cents a dozen; women's wrappers, 49 cents a dozen. Contractors were paid for children's jackets 6⅔ cents apiece, and for knee pants from 4 cents to 8 cents apiece, the workmen receiving less, as the contractor was entitled to his profit. Because of these incredibly low prices, which might be termed dying wages rather than living wages, workers were forced to live huddled together in crowded rooms which served as workrooms as well as living rooms. We sent a copy of the report of our investigations to Theodore Roosevelt, who was at that time Governor of the State of New York; whereupon he, with his usual virile courage and his broad sympathies, decided to attack the problem at once. He came from Albany especially to visit some of the sweatshops, to see for himself actual conditions, stopping first at the office of the Consumers' League in order to get a guide and a list of the worst sweatshops. After his tour of investigation, Governor Roosevelt incorporated into his message to the Legislature a plea for better enforcement of existing labour laws, and suggested further legislation, looking to the ultimate abolition of "the uneconomic, unwholesome, and un-American sweatshop system from our industrial life."[1]

The public began to respond to the efforts of the League to change conditions of production. Retail dealers were quick to feel the pulse of the shopping public. One prominent firm placed tags on their garments, marked: "Sanitary, non-sweatshop make." In connection with an advertised sale of underwear by another equally prominent firm, a notice in the show window read: "Made by clean, contented, and well-paid people, with plenty of time. No 'song of the shirt' horrors are stitched into our garments." Another leading firm paid to have the following advertisement published in the newspapers:

Baby clothes safe to wear. It is a well-known fact that many garments offered for sale at low prices, and sometimes even the better grades, are manufactured in tenements or other unwholesome places, under conditions that make it hazardous to wear them, especially for infants and small children.

We cannot tell where these goods are to be found, but we can tell you about the other kind—made in light, clean workrooms.

---

[1]See Appendix E for extract from Governor Roosevelt's message, published in the report of the Consumers' League of the City of New York, 1898.

A Sixth Avenue firm advertised that *"nearly* all" the underwear found on their counters was made in their own factories; they did not point out, however, how shoppers could distinguish these garments from the others that were evidently made in sweatshops. The League engaged the services of a former factory inspector to investigate factories where women's and children's underwear was made, with a view to ascertaining whether the manufacturers who made these garments under the best conditions on their own premises would use a label authorized by the Consumers' League, thus standardizing their product and suggesting that it be known as the "Consumers' Label." In this way, the shopping public could distinguish these goods from those made under conditions which could not be endorsed by the League. It was found that seventeen out of twenty-two manufacturers interviewed were willing to use a Consumers' League label, *if a demand for it were created.* Such a demand could not be merely local, since the product of factories was distributed throughout the country. With a view, therefore, to creating a widespread demand for such a label, at the suggestion of the Massachusetts Consumers' League, the New York City League invited those leagues which it had helped to establish to send delegates to a convention to discuss the feasibility of forming a national federation of consumers' leagues, one of the duties of which would be to issue a label to standardize conditions in underwear factories.

At this point it might be well to make clear the slight difference in the plan of organization between New

York and other states. Our League, the pioneer league, was known as the Consumers' League of the City of New York, and as other leagues throughout New York State were organized, they took the name of the city or town in which they were formed. In 1898, these various leagues all united under the banner of the New York State Consumers' League. When leagues were formed in other states, they took the name of the state, and all the local leagues organized were considered branches of the State League.

The proposition of the New York League to call a convention met with instantaneous approval. A successful convention was held on May 17 and 18, 1898, representatives from the Brooklyn, Syracuse, New York City, Pennsylvania, Massachusetts, and Illinois leagues being present.

Through the kindness of Rev. J. Lewis Parks, the business sessions were held in Calvary Parish House, where at that time, through Doctor Parks's hospitality, the Governing Board of the New York City League was holding its regular business meetings. The public meeting was held in Assembly Hall, 156 Fifth Avenue, and was largely attended. As president of the Hostess League, I presided and gave an introductory address. Short addresses were made by the presidents of the Pennsylvania and Massachusetts leagues, and for the Illinois League by Mrs. Florence Kelley of Hull House, Chicago. Prof. E. R. A. Seligman of Columbia University, and the late Colonel George E. Waring, Commissioner of the Street-Cleaning Department, New

York City, also addressed the meeting. A resolution was passed recommending a federation of the existing consumers' leagues into a national body.

The newly formed National Consumers' League began its existence with Dr. John Graham Brooks of Cambridge, Massachusetts as president.[1] It opened an office in New York City in May, 1899, and engaged Mrs. Florence Kelley as executive secretary. The secretary was expected to organize new leagues and inspect factories. For more than twenty-five years Mrs. Kelley has been the great driving force behind the manifold activities of the National League. She has veritably become the human embodiment of its aims and principles. In every crusade against vicious national or civic conditions her coöperation has never been lacking. Under the pressure of her energy and her marvellous vitality, her keen intelligence and her power of eloquent expression, local and state consumers' leagues sprang up all over the country, from the State of Washington in the North to Louisiana in the South, from Maine in the East to California in the West. As president of the pioneer league and as first vice-president of the National League, I also had the privilege of helping to sow the seed of many of these new leagues. Whenever I travelled, meetings were arranged and groups of citizens were urged to form a local league to be affiliated with the national body. Each local league was expected to do the work nearest

[1] See Appendix F for the first published list of officers and directors of the National Consumers' League.

at hand to remedy local conditions[1] and was asked also to coöperate in the support of the National League in its endeavour to abolish the sweatshop and its attendant evils.

Some of the trades unions had realized the need of a label in order that their members could distinguish articles made by trade unionists in the "closed shop," but their labels had stood primarily for the fact that all the workers employed in the making of the article were members of the union. The label did not represent necessarily a high standard of conditions, other than those demanded by unions in regard to wages and hours. This label did not guarantee a sanitary environment; indeed, much of the product bearing the union label was known to have been made in tenement rooms. The National Consumers' League felt, therefore, that what was needed was a label that would not only come up to the union standard of wages and hours, but one that would also insure to the purchaser, 1st: sanitary conditions in the production; 2d: a living wage and a fair working day to the producer; 3d: good workmanship; 4th: the elimination of child labour; 5th: the indorsement of the factory inspector; 6th: the privilege of its use by all manufacturers who could prove that they fulfilled the necessary conditions.

It required a great deal of propaganda to create a public opinion which would demand goods bearing our label, and it required as great an effort to induce the manufacturers to place such a label on their garments.

---

[1]See Appendix G for detailed reports of state and local consumers' leagues.

The executive secretary of the National Consumers' League toured the country in order to get the label adopted. I, also, as president of the pioneer league and vice-president of the National League, was invited to address the large gatherings of federated clubs. In my capacity as chairman of the "Committee on Industry of Women and Children" of the General Federation of Women's Clubs, I had the opportunity of bringing the facts before the organized women of the country. The work was strenuous and arduous, but the enthusiastic response that we met was our great encouragement. Finally the White Label was accepted by a few of the manufacturers of women's white underwear. This branch of industry, we found, had the largest percentage of underpaid, undernourished workers, so we decided to begin our work with this particular branch of the needle trades. A contract was drawn up between the manufacturers and the National Consumers' League[1] which covered what we considered the salient points. The first list of recommended manufacturers published contained the names of fifteen firms.[2] During the first year, the economic value of this label was so strongly felt that other groups of manufacturers *asked* to be permitted to sign the contracts and use the label. These groups included makers of corsets, sheets, and pillow cases, curtains, skirt and stocking supporters, shirt waists, and children's wash dresses. The factories using the label were scattered through the following states: Maine, Massachusetts,

[1] See Appendix H for agreement.
[2] See Appendix I for first White Label List.

Michigan, Pennsylvania, and Rhode Island. This product found its way into every corner of the country, and our label was found in Mexico City and in Juneau, Alaska. Our list grew rapidly; we met with the same experience with which we had formerly met in the growth of the White List of New York retail stores. Factories had to be investigated each year to see whether they maintained the required standards; a few had to be dropped occasionally, new names were added until, in 1914, we had a list of sixty-eight firms. Some of these manufacturers turned out 20,000 garments a day.[1] In 1901, there was such a variety of garments being sold which bore the Consumers' League label, that Mrs. Henry B. Sleeper of Worcester, Massachusetts, conceived the idea of making a collection of sample garments which could be purchased with the label attached.

The first exhibition of labelled goods, held in Worcester, created sufficient interest to warrant its being followed by an exhibition held during three days at the Women's Educational and Industrial Union of Boston some months later, after which it was sent to Wellesley College.

This was but the beginning of a series of exhibits held all over the country, being sent actually into

---

[1] In 1918, the Consumers' League discontinued the use of the White Label. Legislation in many states, through the pressure of public opinion, had secured standards even higher than the requirements established by the League for the use of the label.

The Joint Board of Sanitary Control has recently adopted a "Prosanis" label, which is placed on women's dresses and coats, indicating a high standard of manufacture.

twenty-eight states, under the able chairmanship of Mrs. Charles E. H. Phillips. The exhibit contrasted goods made in model factories with those made in tenement sweatshops. The New York League did a large part of the work in collecting samples of sweatshop goods, and the Massachusetts League furnished many samples of labelled underwear.

Placards in the exhibits showed the wages, hours, and conditions of sweatshop workers, as well as of workers in factories.

The exhibit of the National Consumers' League was constantly being enlarged, specimens of foods being added to the list of garments and fancy articles. One specimen of so-called strawberry jam was found not to contain a single strawberry.

I must relate here two incidents which will illustrate the value that the manufacturers in general placed on our label. A firm using the White Label called our attention to the fact that one of his competitors, whose standards fell far below his, was yet permitted to use the label and, because of these low standards, was able to undersell him. We investigated and found that the firm in question, not having been authorized to use the label, had forged it. A lawsuit followed, and the offending firm was forced to abandon the illegally acquired label. Another firm, known all over the world for its 57 varieties, wrote and asked why, in view of the fact that their work was done under conditions that came up to the required standards of the League, they should not be permitted to place the label on their products. The answer was obvious. Though pickles might be as dear to the heart of the American woman as white underwear, by no stretch of the imagination could even one of these 57 varieties be construed to come within the category of the needle trades! Although we treated this request as a laughing matter and were obliged to refuse it, the incident gave us a new idea of the value of the label and of its force in the economic world. We refused it to "pickles," but the time came when the placing of our label on a milk bottle was the means of saving the lives of hundreds of babies.

Two of the local leagues, one in the Middle West and one in the Far West, used their influence and the power of their organizations to compel dairymen to raise their standard of hygiene and sanitation. They conducted such a spirited and vigorous campaign that they were able to get the support of the general public. When dairymen found that the public would only purchase bottles of milk and cream which bore the Consumers' League label, they were soon impressed with the importance of cleaning up their dairies and improving their conditions. In this campaign, the Consumers' League in one city had the staunch support of one of the leading newspapers. It published an article stating that 618 babies less than a year old had died during the year, and that tuberculous or dirty milk had been the cause of nearly every death. Because of the strong public opinion aroused, a city ordinance relating to the inspection and maintenance of dairies and the regulation of the sale of milk and cream was passed, in spite of the opposition of the Dairymen's Association. Thirteen years later, there were in that city but seventeen deaths from diarrhœa and enteritis, of infants less than two years of age.

Another striking and dramatic illustration of the power of the consumer to change conditions was shown in another Western city. The telephone girls asked for higher wages, shorter hours, and better general conditions. The telephone company refused to grant their demands. The girls then went on strike. The company secured temporary help from near-by towns. The newspapers gave publicity to the working conditions of the telephone girls and to their demands. These demands appealed to the public as being just and fair. One morning, through concerted action, the telephone company received notice over the wires from one subscriber after another that, if the demands of the telephone girls were not acceded to, the subscriber wished the telephone removed and the service discontinued. The situation was so startling and unlooked-for that there could be but one response—the girls were taken back on their own terms.

Through our investigations of tenement-made garments in New York we found that not only were germ-laden garments being widely distributed, but also certain processes in food products were being carried on, to the menace of the health of the community, in these same tenement hovels. Nuts were being picked by diseased workers and piled on dirty floors; poisonous chemicals were being used to colour delectable-looking candies; ice cream was being made from impure milk in corroded tins; macaroni was being made in a small room where the worker's child lay sick with diphtheria.

Cellar bakeries, conducted at night in order that fresh loaves might be sold in the morning, were often used in winter as warm sleeping quarters, the kneading-boards serving as beds for the tired workers. While on one tour of inspection we even found a cat snugly reposing on a cushion-like mass of soft dough.

Eleven years after, a law was passed prohibiting cellar bakeries. Three thousand and seventy-seven of these were still flourishing in New York,[1] and this number did not include basement bakeries. The legal differentiation between a cellar bakery and a basement bakery being that the former is *more* than half underground and the latter *less* than half underground.

Committees were formed in the various leagues to investigate further into the matter of prepared-food production, and these committees coöperated with other organizations which were specially interested in this branch of work. It was found that in New York City alone there were 1,360,824 pounds of food seized and condemned within thirteen weeks of the year 1904.

Up to this time, in the licensing of tenements for purposes of manufacture, only wearing apparel had been considered, but, as a result of these investigations, the New York Labour Commissioner introduced a bill into the State Legislature which included food preparations among the articles permitted to be manufactured only in *licensed* tenements. It was not until February, 1906, that the United States Senate passed the Heyburn Pure Food Bill, which aimed to secure to the people of

[1]From report of Committee on Region Plan of New York and its environs.

the country the prevention of "the manufacture, sale, or transportation of adulterated or misbranded or poisonous foods, drugs, medicines, and liquors and regulate traffic therein."

The relating of our investigations in regard to the preparation of food products brings me naturally to the story of restaurant waitresses, who had neither the protection of the factory laws nor of the mercantile laws. In 1916, the New York Consumers' League made an intensive study of the conditions under which these girls worked. More than a thousand women were interviewed, and it was found that fifty-eight per cent. of the girls employed in restaurants worked more than fifty-four hours a week, the legal hours for factories and stores. There was an extreme case in which a girl of twenty years of age worked 122 hours a week. Twenty per cent. worked twelve hours a day and 4 per cent. were employed at night. One third did not have one day of rest in seven, and the majority were not allowed time off for their meals. Work in restaurants, as in stores, entailed almost continuous standing or walking, and serving many customers caused nervous strain. The waitresses began their day at 7 A. M., walked many miles during the day, carrying heavy trays, and reached their homes not earlier than 8 P. M. Usually, there was laundry work to be done in preparation for the next day's service.

Based on the findings of our investigation, we demanded legislation to protect these girls from exploitation. We carried on a vigorous educational campaign urging enactment of a measure which, through our initiative, had been introduced. In 1917, the bill passed both houses and received the Governor's signature, thus emancipating from a species of industrial slavery a group of women who, through broken-down health, would probably have been thrown upon the community for care.

The method employed by the Consumers' League to better conditions invariably followed this rule: obtain facts through investigation, acquaint the public with the facts, and after educating public opinion, secure legislation. We began by interesting ourselves in saleswomen, we enlarged the scope of our work gradually, making not only the investigations already cited, but also in the artificial flower industry, public laundries, silk factories, telephone operators, and hotel employees. The National Consumers' League also made a study of the standard of living of the average factory worker and saleswoman not living at home.

It also played an important rôle in preparing the defence to uphold labour laws declared to be unconstitutional. Out of fifteen cases argued before courts of last resort, there were fourteen decisions favourable to the Consumers' League. Of these, nine were in regard to hours of labour. The League had the valuable assistance of Mr. Louis D. Brandeis, who generously gave his services as counsel to the League until he was appointed to the bench of the United States Supreme Court. After that Mr. Felix Frankfurter was equally generous in contributing his services. Miss Josephine Goldmark, who was one of the staff of the National

League, did magnificent work in preparing the briefs for the arguments.

The New York League coöperated with the Russell Sage Foundation in carrying on an investigation of the cannery industry. Some of the conditions were found to be deplorable: children under ten years of age shelling peas at an hour close upon midnight; in one instance, a little tot had actually fallen asleep with the peapod clutched in his little hand; abnormally long hours during short seasons of work, women sometimes working until 4 A. M. and reporting again for work at 8 A. M. the same day. The canners claimed that it was not possible to secure enough workers in order to enable them to have two shifts; they contended that, as their products were seasonal and perishable, they could do nothing to shorten hours or lengthen seasons of work. So, when protective legislation was enacted, certain exceptions were made in favour of the canning industry. Thus, rather than allow material for manufacture to deteriorate and let the manufacturing interests suffer, women and children were exploited. Dr. Abraham Jacobi, in his plea before a committee hearing in the Capitol at Albany, said sarcastically: "The freshness of the strawberry must be preserved, even if the children of the next generation perish!"

In the investigation of the artificial flower industry it was found that a large percentage of the workers were young Italian children who worked in their homes with their mothers. They worked before and after school hours, sometimes late into the night and also on

Saturdays and Sundays. Their small fingers could often shape the flowers less clumsily than their elders could.

An interesting story is connected with the New York City League's investigation of public laundries. In order to obtain accurate information, Carola Woerishoffer, one of the Governing Board and also a member of the Committee on Investigations, gave up a summer abroad with her mother and took a position, instead, in a laundry; as soon as she had learned, from personal experience, what the conditions were in one laundry, she would leave and secure a position in another. She found the hours very irregular and often very long; she worked sometimes seventeen hours in a day, remaining at work occasionally as late as 2 A. M. and returning at seven o'clock on the same morning. Most of the work had to be done standing; the washroom floors were wet and many of the rooms filled with steam. In the rooms where the machine ironing was done, the heat was excessive. Dangerous machines were left unguarded; wages were low and were paid on a regular weekly pay-day. If a worker left a laundry before this pay-day her wages were not given her; she was obliged to wait for the regular pay-day before receiving them. This often involved great hardship; not only was the money needed, but the worker lost valuable working time in going to collect what was due her.

Too much cannot be said in appreciation of Carola Woerishoffer's devotion to her ideals of altruism. She was a Bryn Mawr graduate, a girl whose life had been surrounded by every comfort and luxury; she had had all the opportunities of education, travel, and culture; she felt so strongly the call to devote these advantages to helping others that she deliberately chose, in place of a summer of pleasure and ease, one of intense heat and hardship, unlovely surroundings, uncongenial companionship, and a strain of physical endurance that nothing but the crusader's spirit that flamed within her would have enabled her to live through. But she did live through it, and the detailed report[1] which she submitted to our Governing Board was the lever that raised the standards of conditions for this branch of workers. The League invited the presidents of the Manhattan and Brooklyn Laundrymen's Associations to a conference in order to frame a fair standard of requirements for a White List of laundries. This White List was to include only those laundries which had guarded machinery, adequate fire protection, proper sanitary conditions, paid not less than $6 a week (for employees eighteen years of age or over and who had had one year's experience), and exacted not more than ten hours' work a day.[2]

The zeal of the Governing Board of the New York City League can be measured by the story of how another member became a factory worker in order to obtain positive knowledge as to the working conditions of a certain silk factory. The factory inspector reported that no evidence of violation of law could be found, yet we had received information to the contrary

---

[1]This report was published in collaboration with Edith Wyatt, in *McClure's Magazine*, issue of February, 1911.

[2]See Appendix O for full text of requirements submitted.

from employees. Louise Lockwood volunteered to secure the evidence. Very early on a cold winter's morning, dressed in the shabbiest skirt she could find, in an ill-fitting thin jacket, a tam-o'shanter cap on her head, no furs, no gloves, she applied for work at the factory. The manager's sympathies were aroused by the appearance of this shivering, poorly clad creature, and she was given a job at once. It did not take this inexperienced "factory hand" long to discover why the factory inspector was unable to find any evidence of violation of law. For when the signal was given that a factory inspector was about to make the rounds of the floors, many ingenious ruses were openly employed to throw dust in the eyes of the credulous inspector. The factory in question had a very bad reputation among working girls; the machines were not kept in good repair and therefore did not turn out a smooth product; yet whenever there was a flaw in the material woven, the girls were heavily fined. They were actually made to pay for a certain amount of goods, although the goods were not given to them. Because of unfair treatment and unfair regulations, the firm was unable to keep employees for any length of time. Perhaps that was one reason that the manager was only too glad to employ an applicant who stated frankly that she was inexperienced. This firm obtained a medal at the Pan-American Exposition held in Buffalo in 1901. The display of silks was unusually attractive; the quality of the goods was admirable, but that a firm which had been known to have been prosecuted by the state factory inspector for violation of state laws was permitted to purchase valuable space at the Exposition and was awarded a medal aroused my indignation. When I was invited to speak at the New York State Building in the Exposition Grounds, I took as my theme the desirability in the future of refusing medals, and even refusing space at exhibits, to firms who violated state laws and who were known to treat their employees unfairly. I pointed out that expositions were futile and a mere waste of energy and money, unless it could be shown that the industrial activities of a nation were carried on in a way to produce, not only good material, but good citizens as well. Of what avail was it to boast of the growth of the commerce and industry of a nation if one could not also be proud of the progress of working conditions, which enabled the people of a democracy to live according to a high standard?

This meeting was attended by many prominent residents of Buffalo, some of whom became so interested in the work of the League that other meetings were arranged, with a view to organizing a Buffalo local league, and the women managers of the Exposition tendered a reception in the Woman's Building to the speakers and members of the New York League.

The Consumers' League of New York was greatly disappointed at being unable to secure a booth at the Buffalo Pan-American Exposition. We wanted to exhibit sweatshop-made articles, showing prices paid, the working hours, unsanitary conditions, etc., side by side with an exhibit of the White Label underwear made in model factories, according to the League's standards of work. We were ready to pay for such space, but the Director General of the Exposition refused to grant us the space, as some of the exhibitors protested. They claimed that our exhibit, with silent eloquence, would emphasize an invidious discrimination. So we were obliged to content ourselves by merely distributing pamphlets and leaflets describing the League's aims and principles. This we were enabled to do from Wisconsin, Illinois, and Ohio buildings, because of pressure brought to bear by the consumers' leagues of those states. In the Liberal Arts Building we had the co-operation of the Wellesley College exhibit, and from the New York State Building our literature was distributed on the day of our public meeting. It is a notable fact that, although the Consumers' League met with opposition and was refused space for its exhibit at the Pan-American Exposition, the National Consumers' League exhibit had been accepted one year previously at the Paris Exposition and a gold medal awarded it by the jury. This award had been made because the League exhibit had shown so clearly and dramatically what it had accomplished and what it was aiming to accomplish.

In 1905, when the Liège (Belgium) International Exposition awarded a gold medal to me as president of the New York City League, I realized that the award was a recognition of the work accomplished by the League I represented. I cite these instances as marking a strong contrast to the policy of the directors of the exposition held in our own state.

In 1906, the League sent an exhibit to the Lewis and

Clark Exposition in Portland, Oregon. Later on, we had exhibits at other expositions in our country; at the Louisiana Purchase Exposition, at St. Louis, we received Honourable Mention. In 1915, the National Consumers' League exhibited twenty-one screens at the Panama-Pacific Exposition held in San Francisco. The following year the exhibit was shown at the Southern Sociological Congress. The League also received a medal for the exhibit shown at the Safety Exposition, because of its work in having protected and saved the lives of so many thousands of working girls. These awards came as a climax to the campaign of education we had been carrying on for some time, by installing exhibits wherever opportunity was afforded us. We placed them in vacant stores, when progressive landlords allowed us to use them while they were untenanted; we showed the relationship of our work to tuberculosis by exhibiting at the International Tuberculosis Exhibition. Our relation to problems of overcrowding and of housing was shown by the exhibit we prepared for the Exhibit of Congestion of Population. The New York Consumers' League exhibit had been sent throughout the state, to schools and colleges, to county fairs and to conventions of welfare organizations, and conventions of the Federation of Labour and of women's clubs. Requests for the exhibit came from other states, and it was because these requests became so numerous that it was found necessary for the National Consumers' League to have its own exhibit for interstate and international purposes.

It is a pedagogic truism that knowledge acquired

through the medium of the eye makes a deeper impression than knowledge acquired through the medium of the ear. But it has only been of recent years that the public has come to accept this. The Consumers' League was quick to adopt this new method of teaching. Lantern slides, exhibits, and moving pictures were gradually utilized to supplement speeches and distribution of literature. The public conscience was being quickened, stimulated, and made more sensitive along many lines. We in America have criticized and condemned the system by which the absentee landlord of England's great landed estates can sit in the House of Lords and draw his large income from homes on his estate that are almost uninhabitable. He dispenses his largesse with a generous hand while his tenants suffer from leaky roofs and ill-kept drains. Some of the directors of the National Consumers' League were startled into a realization that the position of the stockholder drawing his large income from industrial dividends with huge "melons" cut semi-annually is analogous to that of the English landed gentry. These industrial dividends are frequently all the higher, and the melons cut all the larger, because of low wages and unfair working conditions. That the investor, drawing income from such dividends, has the power vested in the consumer, can be forcibly illustrated by the following incident:

The National Consumers' League received a request from one of its members asking that it issue a White List of industrials having their stocks or bonds on the market. This correspondent pointed out that many people did not wish to invest their money while in ignorance of the working conditions under which dividends were produced. It was suggested that industries should be listed by the League in regard to working hours, wages, sanitary surroundings, heat, light, ventilation, etc. The writer of the letter sent a check for $1,000 as an earnest of his conviction that the Consumers' League was adequate to the task. This incident sets forth the power of the investor and shows how the propaganda in the education of public opinion had brought forth the conviction that, if high standards were demanded, conditions could be changed.

While the National Consumers' League never published a "White List of Industrial Investments," it considered that its White List of manufacturers using the label, while limited in scope, served as an index and opening wedge in this direction. Several instances came to our notice in which stockholders in large corporations demanded that standards of working conditions be raised to the level of Consumers' League principles. In other instances, those imbued with the ideals of the League declined to become stockholders in certain Southern cotton mills, where dividends were high but working conditions notoriously low.

Into the busy, swirling whirlpool of New York's social and industrial life an idea was flung—a pebble which seemed scarcely to ruffle the surface of the current. Yet it took the usual natural course; in reality, it plumbed the depths and the resulting circles widened and ever widened, until at last the opposite shore was reached.

From one City Consumers' League to ninety local leagues; from one State Consumers' League to twenty state leagues; from one college branch to thirty-five college and school branches; from one auxiliary Consumers' League to thirty-five auxiliary leagues; from a National Consumers' League to an International Conference of American and Foreign Consumers' Leagues was but a natural expansion.

CHAPTER V

> Vivre, c'est acheter; acheter, c'est pouvoir; pouvoir, c'est devoir. (To live means to buy, to buy means to have power, to have power means to have duties.)—*Maxim of the First International Conference of Consumers' Leagues.*

THE ideals and principles of the Consumers' League originally came to us from England, but tradition and conservatism are forces against which it is difficult to battle, and the League languished in the country which had given it birth. In 1899, it was practically non-existent. However, the Women's Industrial Union of England, an association identical in its aims with the Working Women's Society of New York, was endeavouring to remedy certain abuses in industry. Its attention had been called to the working conditions of "shop assistants."[1] Their hours were long, they had no seats behind counters; the invariable rule which compelled employees to wear black silk or satin dresses, the cost of which they were obliged to defray from their low wages, constituted a hardship. A bill to regulate these conditions had been introduced into the House of Commons and had passed that body. When the bill reached the House of Lords, it was held up, this august

---

[1] Saleswomen in England are termed "shop assistants."

body declaring solemnly that if such protection were given shop assistants, the next step would be a demand to regulate household service. The committee considering the bill also claimed that such a bill was not practical because it was not possible of enforcement. Miss Clementina Black and other leaders of the Women's Industrial Union knew that a law protecting saleswomen had been passed in New York State and was being enforced. This information was given to the aforesaid committee. The chairman of the committee, the Marquis of Salisbury, asked Joseph H. Choate, who was at that time the United States Ambassador at the Court of St. James's, if he could secure for him a copy of this law and a statement of its working practicability. Mr. Choate, having no data at hand, asked Mrs. Josephine Shaw Lowell, who happened to be in London at the time, if she had a copy of the Mercantile Law of New York State. He also wanted information as to the enforcement of the law.

Mrs. Lowell did not have the required data with her and referred Mr. Choate to me, saying: "If you cannot procure a copy of the law from Mrs. Nathan, who is also in London, I fear you will have to send to New York for it." I was abroad that year, having been invited to address the Quinquennial Congress of the International Council of Women, which was to be held in London that spring. I had brought with me various data, records, etc., to be used as reference in making my address, and a copy of the Mercantile Law was among these papers. I was very glad to be able to place it at Mr. Choate's service. The Marquis of

Salisbury, upon asking for further details as to its enforcement, was referred to me. I was invited to appear
before the Committee of the House of Lords to state
what I knew as to the feasibility and practical enforcement of this law. I was thrilled at the wonderful opportunity that opened before me, I felt the necessity of
presenting my facts well in order to lighten the burden
of the British shop-girl as we had succeeded in easing
it for the New York shop-girl. I felt that the responsibility was tremendous, and perhaps my excitement
and nervousness, added to the fatigue of a strenuous
London season, may have been one of the causes of an
acute attack of tonsillitis which prevented me from
presenting my case personally. However, I wrote a
very full and detailed report, which I sent to the Chairman of the Committee. Shortly afterwards I had the
supreme satisfaction of reading in the London *Times*
that the Shop Assistants' Act had passed in the House of
Lords and was to go into effect the following September. I had the further satisfaction of seeing the Act enforced in Glasgow, before I sailed for home. Apropos
of this incident, Mr. Choate, whose epigrams were
famous, said to me: "I congratulate you, madam: you,
an American, are the first woman to have knocked on
the doors of the historic House of Lords and to have
had them opened for you."

I have already referred to the Quinquennial Congress
that was being held in London during the spring of 1899.
This international body was made up of delegates from
national organizations of women throughout the world,
who were interested in educational, social, civic, and eco-

nomic problems. The spirit of these conferences, which were held in different capitals of the Old and New worlds every five years, was one of mutual helpfulness and education along the lines mentioned, with a view of finding a solution for some of these weighty problems. My address, given at an evening session of the convention held at Westminster Town Hall, was on "The Ethics of Money-Making and Money-Spending." The meeting was presided over by Lady Aberdeen, the Marchioness of Aberdeen and Temair, who was at that time the president. I remember that Beatrice Webb also was one of the speakers at that session. It was a rainy evening, and I predicted that there would not be many present. Much to my surprise, when we arrived at the hall, it was so crowded that the police told us we could not get in. Only my delegate's badge and the assurance that I was one of the speakers procured us an entrance. The overflow crowd was so great that it was decided to throw open the smaller hall in the same building, and the speakers were requested to repeat the addresses there. Mrs. MacDonald presided at the overflow meeting. As soon as the doors were opened, the seats were at once filled and the police had the same difficulty in keeping the crowd outside from overflowing the aisles —or the gangways, as they are called in England—as they had had outside of the larger hall. I mention this to show how much public interest was evinced in the congress, for even on a rainy evening, when the subjects for discussion pertained to what was considered a dry topic—Economics—the crowd was almost unmanageable. This crowd was made up, not only of people interested in the congress, and their immediate friends, but scattered through the throngs were seen many leading men of affairs. A few years before, men would have scoffed at the mere suggestion of attending a women's meeting, but now they came to listen, to learn, and we hoped to teach. As I stood up to give my address and looked out over the throng that filled the vast hall, I could not help but recall that the message I was bringing from the New World was but the flowering of the seed that had first been sown in the mother country, and on being successfully transplanted across the sea, its growth had not been hampered by traditions and conventions. Among my listeners was a well-known French writer, the editor of a French revue; I think her name was Madame Blanc. She was so impressed with the facts which I presented in the course of my address, relating to the principles and aims of the Consumers' League, that she took copious notes and, translating them into French, published them in her revue. The following winter the New York Consumers' League received requests from Paris for our reports, leaflets, etc. These were translated and published in the French revue. However, it was not until the summer of 1903, when I was "taking a cure" at Aix-les-Bains, that, following a correspondence with Professor and Madame Jean Brunhes, they decided to visit me, in order to talk over the feasibility of starting a French consumers' league. Professor Jean Brunhes occupied a chair at the University of Fribourg, and he and his wife travelled for several hours at night in a day coach for two nights in succession, in order to have a long interview with me and return to Fribourg the same day. The interview lasted two and a quarter hours. The following winter "La Ligue Social ed'Acheteurs"—as the French league was called—was organized with head-quarters in Paris.[1] The directors felt that their most important work lay in regulating the abuses relating to overtime work and Sunday work in the *"établissements de couturières, modistes, et lingères."* "La Ligue Sociale d'Acheteurs" of Paris issued White Lists (*des Listes Blanches*) of those firms which agreed in writing: 1st: Not to work their employees normally later than 7 P. M., and never, even in rush seasons, later than 9 P. M., 2d: Not to give work to their employees on Sundays. The League called upon its members, 1st: Not to give any orders without satisfying themselves that the carrying out of the orders would not entail overtime or Sunday work; 2d: to avoid giving orders at the last moment, especially during rush seasons; 3d: To refuse all deliveries made after 7 P. M. or on Sundays, so as not to be indirectly responsible for prolonging the working hours for delivery clerks, employees, or apprentices; 4th: To pay their bills regularly and promptly.

The American consumers' leagues were called upon to coöperate with their new French sister league, and bundles of *Listes Blanches* were distributed among the fifty-seven leagues which at that time had been or-ganized in the United States, so that any members who contemplated going abroad would know at what es-tablishments in Paris they could conscientiously pur-chase their gowns, their hats, and their underwear.

---

[1]See Appendix J for first published list of officers and directors.

These lists were also distributed on some of the trans-
atlantic steamers. It was a well-known fact that much
of the overtime and Sunday work in Paris *établissements*
was caused by the thoughtlessness of American shoppers, who persisted in giving orders within a few days
of their sailing for home. They often insisted upon
having completed in a few days what would take them
as many weeks to have made at home. The Paris
League related that it had received a pathetic letter from
a dressmaker's employee, stating that she and the other
girls were forced to work until *midnight* to complete a
dress hurriedly for an American lady, and that their
mothers had been distracted when they did not reach
their homes until 1 A. M., knowing the danger of Paris
streets at night. Moreover, American women, who,
when at home, would not think of shopping of an evening or on Sundays, when abroad went, with light hearts,
souvenir-hunting without regard to hours or the customary day of rest. They did not realize that they were
the means of preventing storekeepers of small stores
from closing early or from granting even one day of rest
to their employees.

While there is no necessity to enter into the growth
of the French Consumers' League from its beginnings
in Paris until it had twenty-eight branches throughout
France, its inception is an interesting chapter in the
history of our expansion. However, one story which
will illustrate the force of an educated public opinion
may well be told here. Professor Maurice Deslandres
of the University of Dijon was vice-president of the
French Consumers' League. He awoke one Sunday

morning to find that no bread had been delivered in
Dijon that day. There was a strike of bakers' delivery
boys. The boys had felt that it was an imposition not
to have one day of rest a week. The proprietors of
the bakeries protested that because their customers demanded freshly baked bread and rolls on Sundays, it
was impossible for them to give the delivery boys a day
off. Professor Deslandres at once began educating
the public at Dijon. He insisted that the boys were
entitled to their one day of rest, and proclaimed that
consumers should demand that their bread for use on
Sundays be baked and delivered on Saturdays. He
suggested that the power and influence of the French
Consumers' League would be behind the striking employees. So, although there was but a handful of
League members in Dijon, the realization that a body
of well-known men and women was interested in their
welfare was sufficient to enable the boys to win their
strike. The educational campaign led by Professor
Deslandres was the means of arousing public sentiment
to such a degree that a large number of people joined
the League and agreed to have their bread delivered on
Saturdays, or else call at the bakeries for the loaves,
themselves, on Sunday mornings.

Another interesting piece of work accomplished by
the French League was the opening of workrooms for
the benefit of the many working girls who were without
employment during dull seasons. In these workrooms
candle shades were made, lamp shades, and other
articles which did not go out of style quickly. Lace
curtains were repaired, and members of the League

were asked to send their curtains there before leaving Paris for the summer.

The little seed sown at the convention in London in the spring of 1899 was destined to reap a further harvest. Madame Jean Brunhes spent part of each year in Switzerland with her husband, therefore, she was also interested in the welfare of Swiss working girls; she was the secretary of the French League, and its most ardent worker, yet she decided to help form a Swiss league as well. She became the inspiring genius of both leagues. No one was more zealous, more conscientious, more devoted to the cause. Her untimely death in 1914 was no doubt due to some extent to the burning up of her stamina and vitality through the inextinguishable fire of her enthusiasm, and her desire to abolish unjust conditions for the weak and oppressed. Truly, those who fight the enemy with shot and shell in times of war are not the only heroes, and those who succumb are not the only martyrs. Those who, like Henriette Brunhes, battle for the right in campaigns waged between capital and labour, in times of peace, with many obstacles to overcome, show heroic fortitude, and when at last their weakened bodies succumb, their spirits live to inspire others to take up the weapons and wield them in defence of the cause.

The Swiss Consumers' League[1] concerned itself first with trying to raise the standard of conditions in factories. It investigated chocolate factories and published a list of those where standards of conditions met with its approval. From the manufactured product

[1]See Appendix K for first list of officers and directors.

back to the methods employed to secure the cocoa bean was but a natural step. The Swiss League accomplished a wonderful piece of educational work in arousing public opinion in regard to cruelties perpetrated in the West African Islands of San Thome and Principe in the employment of slave labour. These islands produced about one sixth of the world's cocoa crop. The Swiss League also placed a white label on knitted goods made in model factories, and asked the coöperation of other leagues in creating a demand for these garments. The Swiss League, with headquarters in Berne, succeeded in organizing ten branch leagues in the various cantons.

It was at the Quinquennial Convention of the International Council of Women, held in Berlin in 1904, that I gave an address in German on "The Consumers' League." As a result, I was able to interest a group of German delegates who realized the necessity of forming a similar organization in their own country. They translated our name literally, calling the Association "Der Liga von Konsumenten,"[1] afterwards changed to "Der Kaüferbund." I went with the leaders of the movement to visit some of the Berlin department stores, and the League started its work by trying to raise standards in all stores to the level of the few which were placed on its White List. The German League also endeavoured to abolish child labour in cottage industries and to regulate these cottage industries in such a way as to shorten the very long hours of work for women, and prolong the short working seasons.

[1] See Appendix L for first list of officers and directors.

One of the earliest foreign leagues to be formed was The Dutch Consumers' League,[1] but it was only in existence a few years.

In 1908 the French League conceived the idea that it would be mutually helpful to hold an International Conference of Consumers' Leagues. So the National Consumers' League of the United States, concurring in the idea, delegated its general secretary, Mrs. Florence Kelley, and its first vice-president, myself, to attend the conference, as the National League's official representatives. It is interesting to note that, having decided to hold this conference in Geneva, Switzerland, the University of Geneva through the courtesy of the Superintendent of Public Education, threw open wide its doors and invited us to hold our meetings within its halls. This was in September, 1908. Monsieur Auguste de Morsier, deputy of le Grand Conseil from the Canton of Vaux, presided at the meetings. At this conference there were delegates from France, Switzerland, Germany, England, Belgium, Italy, Austria, Spain, and the United States. This does not mean that consumers' leagues had been formed in all the countries named, but it does mean that there were groups of people in all these countries sufficiently interested to warrant their sending delegates. From England the delegates came from the Anti-sweating League; from Italy came delegates from a consumers' league which had been organized the previous year and was still feeble; from Germany came not only delegates from the German Consumers' League but also

[1] See Appendix L for first list of officers and directors.

from the German Home-workers' Union.   The keynote of the Conference was struck by the motto which was printed on all the literature distributed by the Conference: "*Vivre, c'est acheter; acheter, c'est pouvoir; pouvoir, c'est devoir.*"

The National Consumers' League and the League of New York City coöperated in the preparation of a special exhibit which was taken to Geneva for this International Conference.   We had signs attached to all the articles showing in three languages the conditions under which they had been made in sweatshops and in approved factories.   There were similar exhibits which had been prepared by the French, Swiss, and German leagues, and the prices paid the workers for some of these articles were even lower than those paid in the United States.   This was due to the fact that the cost of living was lower in those countries.   Although our conference had been preceded earlier in the season by several other international congresses held in Geneva, it had the largest attendance of any, and claimed the largest number of members.   Among the distinguished men and women who took active part in the discussions were members of the French Academy and of the French Institute, professors of the College of Social Science of Paris, professors of the Universities of Paris, of Dijon, of Rennes, of Fribourg and of Lausanne, members of the Academy of Moral and Political Sciences, Counsellor of State and Chief of the Department of Labour, Paris, one of the inspectors of labour from Bourg-la-Reine, the vice-president of the Society of Agriculturists of France, and two members of the

Anti-sweating League of London. The Bureau of Health of the Canton of Geneva officially joined the congress. At the opening session the chief of the Department of Public Instruction, and the state and administrative councillors extended, in the name of the canton and city of Geneva, a cordial welcome to the delegates and members of the congress.

Notwithstanding the success of the congress, no international league was organized, as it was considered more important that each national league should work for the betterment of industrial conditions and for the education of consumers in its own country, along whatever lines of reform seemed most desirable. It was hoped that at some future day, not too distant, we might succeed in establishing good conditions, good labour laws, and a high standard of ethics for consumers in all countries, by helping each other maintain the highest standard of conditions the world over. We were widely separated, scattered over two continents, but with our present commercial relations, with our great steamship travel, our world newspapers, our system of wireless telegraphy and telephony, and our airships, we felt that we were drawing closer and closer together, and that less than ever ought there to be any desire to exploit the workers of neighbouring nations.

Resolutions[1] were passed at the Conference, with a view to promoting the moralization of industry and the hastening of the day when work would no longer spell drudgery, darkness, disease, despair for many, but

[1] See Appendix M for a free translation of the resolutions passed.

through enlightenment and progress, would become the hope, the benefaction, the redemption of humanity.

One of the direct results of the International Conference was the organization of the Belgian Consumers' League, with headquarters in Antwerp.[1] The guiding spirits of the Belgian League were: Madame la Baronne T. Osy de Zegwaart, Madame H. Belpaire, Madame la Duchesse d'Ursel, and Madame Neuckens. The League became very active and, early in 1913, sent an invitation to all the other leagues to meet in conference in Antwerp a second time the following September. In response to this invitation Mrs. Kelley and I were again delegated to represent the National Consumers' League of the United States. It was felt that these international conferences gave impetus to the younger leagues and that all the leagues derived profit from an interchange of views and experiences. Again Monsieur de Mortsier was elected the presiding officer. There were representatives from the French League, which, at that time, was composed of twenty-five sections, the Swiss League, composed of eleven sections, the German League, of six sections, and the Belgian League, which already boasted of four sections. Reports were sent from leagues in Italy and Spain, which were not financially strong enough to warrant them in sending delegates. The delegates from the United States again took an exhibit to the Conference. The public evening meeting was largely attended. All the speeches were delivered in French, except one given in Flemish by a priest. Among the interested listeners were the

[1] See Appendix N for published list of Provisional Committee.

Governor of the Province, the Mayor of Antwerp, and several of the city councillors. Unfortunately, the following year brought the terrible war which, among the rest of the havoc, shattered the Belgian League and rendered its fine work useless. Since then, the world has been in such a restless state that no further International Consumers' League conferences have been called. In recent years there have been many world conferences on treaties, on armaments, on the right of self-determination, on the best means of abolishing war, but the fundamental economic law of "live and let live" has not been sufficiently emphasized. This simple axiom has been the guiding principle of the Consumers' League idea, and until its force is recognized by the nations, there must always be the spirit of revolt which leads to wars. Some philosopher has said that the key to the solution of all the economic problems of the day is "to make our personal wants at one with the supreme good of the entire universe." It is the consumer who holds the key.

CHAPTER VI

Nothing is done in which there yet remains something to
be done.

—NAPOLEON.

Nearly all the value of life comes from the esteem in which
we hold our fellow men.

—SHALER.

IN MY opening chapter I have tried to show what the
traveller of thirty-five years ago would have seen
upon arriving in New York on a hot Saturday in July or
August. Let us imagine another traveller, a New
Yorker returning to his native city after an absence of
thirty-five years. He, too, arrives on a hot Saturday
in midsummer. What does he find? Driving up the
broad thoroughfare of Fifth Avenue, to him once famous
for its fashionable and exclusive residences, he might
think that he had reached a dead city; at least, a city
dead to the universal need and pastime of womankind
the world over. For the shutters of all the great department stores, as well as the world-famous specialty
shops, which line the Avenue are drawn tightly, doors
are barricaded, and a strange air of quiet and stillness
pervades the scene. Fifth Avenue, Broadway, and
Sixth Avenue—the great, throbbing, pulsing arteries

of the city—do not pulsate with life, the same sense of stillness and calm which pervades a cemetery seems to hover over these great palatial, sartorial, and artistic markets which, during five days of the week, are veritable beehives of activity.

This strange condition, however, does not signify that the merchant princes are dead. On the contrary, it denotes that they are very much alive—alive to the exigencies of the day; that they have acquiesced in the demand of the workers for a fuller, richer life, for a life that includes a week-end in the country during the heated season; that they have succumbed to the power wielded by a conscience-awakened and discriminating public, which recognizes the beneficence of maintaining high standards in industry as a need of the community. The apparent death-like inactivity and stillness of the shopping area of the greatest city in the New World is in reality but the symbol of an awakened public conscience which has been the means of procuring for thousands of nerve-racked beings the opportunity to refresh their bodies and souls, communing with nature in God's open spaces. It is but an illustration of the truism that the symbols of inactivity and death are but the tokens of greater fulness of life elsewhere. If this bewildered New Yorker, who found his erstwhile famous residential Fifth Avenue turned into an equally famous shopping mart, could have delved a little further into the causes of the death-like stillness that pervaded it, he would have found that side by side with the upward march of business from the lower realms of the city had stalked the upward trend of business ideals.

The Consumers' League was not only educating the purchasing public, its spirit was invading the consciousness of employers as well. No longer were we obliged to plead for much-needed reforms. Merchants began to vie with each other in giving more humane attention to the needs of their employees. In the old days saleswomen thought of vacations with a sense of dread. They were days without pay. The employers considered a reduction of the force of clerks a necessary economy during the dull season, whilst priding themselves upon, granting a vacation to their employees. To-day, no self-respecting merchant juggles with his conscience in this wise. A week's vacation with pay is the rule in all first-class establishments, and two weeks with pay are frequently given. The modern merchant considers the welfare of his employees.

A new position has sprung into being: The "Social Secretary" has been ensconced in some of the stores. It is difficult to define her duties; she stands in the relation of "Store Mother" to the girls.

In the old days a working girl could feel no assurance that faithful service and increasing efficiency would receive their due meed of recognition. As an illustration of this I may well tell of an incident which came to the knowledge of the Consumers' League. A department store, moving into larger and showier quarters, advertised for saleswomen, offering what was then considered a weekly wage beyond that of its competitors. Many girls, tempted by the larger salary, left their assured positions and entered the new establishment. After a few weeks, when the éclat incident to the opening of the new store had subsided, these girls were dismissed and cheaper labour employed. This was in the middle of the dull season, when it was difficult to find other employment, and their former positions had been filled by others. To-day a young woman entering a mercantile establishment does so with the reasonable confidence that "if she makes good" and desires to make this her life work, she has every opportunity afforded her for advancement. The progressive merchant of to-day appreciates the value of efficiency in his business and is willing to pay for it. He carries this even to the point of a form of coöperation. A few firms throughout the country have established profit-sharing and have inaugurated a policy of self-government. Employees as well as employers are represented on the Board of Directors of such establishments.

Those who, in recent years, have secured positions in any of the large department stores consider themselves fortunate, for they are able, without deduction of salary, to leave the hot, dusty city on a Friday evening to seek the shelter of green trees in near-by country resorts; to get a dip in the cool surf of the ocean, or to nestle under the protecting wing of some mountain. For department stores—as well as all stores claiming the prestige of being considered first class—have been closed during July and August from Friday at 5 P. M. until Monday at 9 A. M. for the last few years. As in former years, the palatial houses and apartments are closed for the summer months—their owners away: over the seas or at seashore or mountain-side. Now these vacations have a zest which had been lacking in the old days, for to-day these dwellers in luxurious homes, whose wealth and position spell power, have used this power in order to secure for their less fortunate neighbours the opportunity for refreshment of body and soul.

It requires no vivid imagination to depict the enormous difference this one portentous fact of a week-end vacation during two months of the year makes in the lives of thousands—literally hundreds of thousands—of working girls. Although I have specially stressed the benefit of the *working girls*, it must not be overlooked that, when an industrial establishment closes its doors for a week-end holiday, every employee connected with the business benefits. To-day business men realize that the benefit of these week-end holidays accrues not only to the workers, but to their employers, as well; for the employees bring to their work on Monday morning a freshness and zest which make for efficiency and better service. No longer is salesmanship considered "unskilled labour"; there are schools of salesmanship in many of the department stores, and wages, although still low in many stores, considering the rise in the cost of living, yet are considerably higher than the minimum wage demanded by the Consumers' League in its first Standard of a Fair House. Thirty-five years ago it would have been impossible for a society girl to become a shop-girl without feeling that she had lost caste; the conditions of her work were such that she would have been subjected to mortification and humiliation; the physical strain for one gently bred would have been unendurable. To-day, young women of good family and high social position are often found taking such "jobs" in order to gain experience. Employers are glad to engage such young women, realizing that their charm, refinement, and family connections attract custom. No longer are little children seen trudging wearily through the stores, answering the constant cry of "Cash, cash," being paid $1.50 and $2 a week as in former days; to-day there are mechanical contrivances installed in the stores which do the work more rapidly and more economically and efficiently. Legislation enacted prevents any children under sixteen years of age from working in stores without a working certificate, and these certificates are given only to children between the ages of fourteen and sixteen, and only when they have had the required amount of schooling. When youths are employed for errands which cannot be satisfactorily done by machinery, or for messages which cannot be transmitted by telephone, continuation schools are conducted in many department stores, giving these young people opportunity for further educational advantages. No longer is it necessary to drag soap boxes up from a cellar and hide them behind a counter in order to have something to drop upon when overcome with fatigue; now there are seats behind counters, attached to the fixtures so that they cannot be removed. And no longer do floor-walkers consider it "unbusinesslike" to have saleswomen seated until a customer approaches the counter. No longer need a fainting saleswoman be stretched on a concrete floor of a sub-basement. To-day, in the leading department stores, the firms show with pride their fine rest rooms (often on the top floor, with open-air loggia on the roof) including rooms where their employees' teeth can be attended to by a good dentist, their feet cared for by a pedicure, a physician's office where they can consult a good physician, and a trained nurse to care for them if they feel tired or slightly ill. In some stores there are basketball, a piano, magazines, papers, and every luxury. Indeed, such rooms might not unfittingly be compared with the lounge of a social club. There is to be found a well-appointed restaurant in charge of a competent woman where, for a trifling sum, a hot or cold luncheon may be procured, or a beverage served with the luncheon brought from home. These luncheons need not be gulped down, standing with anxious eye fixed on a clock, lest the ten or fifteen minutes be exceeded; to-day there are chairs and tables, and the girls can enjoy their luncheon leisurely, knowing that they have from forty-five minutes to an hour for their meal. Alice in Wonderland could not have been more surprised at some of the things she observed than would be an investigator of the stores who had visited them thirty-five years ago, and who saw them a second time as they are now—such a metamorphosis seems incredible. Indeed, I had such an "Alice in Wonderland-like" experience, myself, when Colonel Michael Friedsam, president of B. Altman & Company, telephoned to me inviting me to visit their new Fifth Avenue store, in all its departments, before it was thrown open to the general public. I accepted the invitation, Colonel

Friedsam personally escorting me through the splendid establishment. I was amazed and delighted at what I was shown. Altman's standards had always been high, and the firm had been among those on our first White List, but the present provision for the comfort, the well-being, the safety of the employees, went far beyond the most optimistic dreams of the Consumers' League. The firm had come to recognize the economic value of the Consumers' League's standards. In asking me, as the president of the League, to inspect the rooms set aside for the comfort and welfare of the employees, it was with the expressed desire for criticism and suggestion. We felt that this was a high tribute to our years of effort, and I am glad of this opportunity to acknowledge our appreciation. It was a further satisfaction to receive a letter from this firm on the occasion of the New York League's twenty-fifth anniversary dinner, requesting the privilege of participating, and asking that a table for ten covers be reserved in the name of the firm. To those of us who remembered the way in which our organization was met in the early days by some of the well-known retail establishments, and the fateful prophecies uttered, this generous recognition of our work came to us as a triumph, and seemed a fitting climax to our twenty-five years of effort.

It is not only the retail firms that have felt the impetus directed by the Consumers' League for better working conditions for employees. Manufacturers also have responded to the new attitude towards those who turn the wheels and tend the machines of their industries. The trade unions have played their part to accomplish this. I recall having heard the story of what has been termed the first working girls' strike in our country. In a certain factory the "hands" worked during an excessively hot summer in the loft of a building where the sun's rays beat upon the roof and streamed through the shutterless windows. The girls pleaded for awnings or for some protection from the intense heat. None was given. One girl after another was overcome by the sizzling atmosphere, became ill, and was obliged to lose some days' work, which meant loss of pay as well. Finally, the girls all agreed to stop work at the same hour, march out of the factory, and refuse to return until awnings had been put up at the windows. The factory owner then realized that through stalled machinery he would lose more than the awnings would cost, so he yielded, grudgingly, to the demands of his workers.

To-day, it is a cause for rejoicing that it would be almost impossible to find a parallel situation. Our factories are not all model factories with the gardens and playgrounds which surround so many of them, but manufacturers do feel a sense of responsibility and duty towards their employees. An effort is made throughout the country to provide good working conditions even beyond those required by law and exacted by trade unions.

The experience of the Consumers' League of New York City led it to realize that factory inspectors should have preliminary training for their work. Through its influence there has been established at Columbia University a course of study, and the executive secretary of the New York League has been appointed instructor of this branch of the Economic Extension Department —the course for labour inspectors. During the first term the students represented eight states of the Union, which clearly shows the widespread demand for experts.

When the Consumers' League began its campaign for early Christmas shopping, we sometimes met women who said: "Oh! *my* few purchases cannot exhaust or break down the health of the shop-girls; besides, I never can determine upon the choice of gifts until I feel the Christmas spirit!" But to-day one woman's club after another has adopted the League's slogan of "Do your Christmas shopping early!" and at the meeting held the first week in December, the president of the club often calls on all those members present to rise if they have finished their Christmas shopping. No member wishes to hurt the reputation of her club by being delinquent, so the individual members have developed the group conscience, and most of these organizations stand as a unit for early Christmas shopping, the various clubs vying with one another in proclaiming their civic virtue. In some of our large cities the traction car companies display on their cars conspicuous placards urging early Christmas shopping. These placards appear immediately after Thanksgiving Day. They are a reminder which cannot be overlooked. These cars running into far-outlying suburbs carry their message to the less alert members of the communities. No longer do shoppers feel that they must wait until the last hurried days before the holiday. To-day early Christmas shopping is recognized as an integral part of the ethics of the mercantile world, by both merchant and consumer. Each year holiday goods are displayed earlier and earlier to meet an ever-increasingly early demand.

It was to us a great source of satisfaction that our point of view became eventually the point of view of our great public carriers—the express companies and the post-office authorities. I have pointed out how, in former days, men were overworked delivering packages during abnormally long hours on the last days of the Christmas holiday season. Our educational campaign asking members, not only to shop early in the season, but also to send their packages well in advance, was taken up later by the express companies in a widespread plea to the general public, with the warning that they could not guarantee delivery of parcels if not sent at an early day. They even supplied customers with "stickers"—"Do not open before Christmas"—to place on packages, giving them gratis, as an inducement to send such packages weeks ahead. When the Consumers' League first appealed to Uncle Sam to allow senders of parcel-post packages to write this plea —"Do not open before Christmas"—on parcels sent in advance of the holiday, it was contended that such an inscription would necessitate sending the package by first-class mail at an extra cost. Later, however, another ruling was obtained, and the following notice was placed, in 1924, in all the city post offices, and as early as November 10th:

CHRISTMAS
MAIL!

Cards—Parcels—Letters

SHOP
and }NOW
MAIL

WRAP PARCELS SECURELY
Address all mail plainly—include street and number

SUPPLY RETURN ADDRESS

Mail may be marked "NOT TO BE OPENED UNTIL
CHRISTMAS"

Postmaster please place conspicuously
JOHN H. BARTLETT
First Assistant Postmaster General.

HARRY S. NEW
Postmaster General.

The Post Office Department realized that efficiency was gained by avoiding the swamping of the Post Office by enormous quantities of mail pouring in during a period of a few days—a week at the most. It had always been necessary to employ extra service or pay extra for overtime work, so the new régime of handling this mail over a period of several weeks, rather than having it concentrated within a few days, has resulted in economy as well as efficiency. The demand to-day for these "stickers"—"Do not open before Christmas"—is so widespread that a well-known manufacturing company makes a specialty of fancy labels and tags to meet this demand.

It is only a few years ago that the Post Office advertised that there would be extra deliveries on Christmas Day, in order to facilitate the distribution of Christmas mail. To-day the postmaster advertises: No mail will be delivered on Christmas Day.

The Post Office is not the only department of the United States Government that has recognized the standards of the Consumers' League. In 1917, Hon. Newton D. Baker was president of the National Consumers' League. He was at that time in President Wilson's Cabinet, serving as Secretary of War. When the United States was forced into the great conflict, Secretary Baker was determined that the War Department should not repeat the mistakes in regard to the making of uniforms that it had made during the time of the Spanish-American War of 1898. The uniforms at that time were given out under the contract system and made in sweatshops. Disease among the soldiers was traced to this fact. During the recent war, Secretary Baker appointed a committee of three (one of them being the General Secretary of the National Consumers' League) to study and control conditions governing the manufacture of army uniforms. The Committee was created in order to uphold and maintain the industrial standards which had been established by the Consumers' League. Secretary Baker knew the dire results that would follow the lowering of standards, even during such a crisis. He had the rare vision which led him to insist that the high standards endorsed by the League should be maintained in regard to the work done under his department for the Government. It is also interesting to note that the United States Government, during the war, adopted the Christmas early-shopping idea, originated by the Consumers' League of the City of New York.   By the use of enormous billboards and other signs, it requested people to shop early as a measure of industrial adjustment.

Again the Consumers' League, in conjunction with the Child Labour Committee, influenced Uncle Sam. The pressure these two organizations brought to bear in the interest of child welfare resulted in the establishment of the Federal Children's Bureau in Washington with Julia Lathrop in charge.   Ida Clyde Clarke says that "Uncle Sam needs a wife."   In the Consumers' League he has found a suggestive and useful helpmate. It is interesting to note the authoritative status of the League's publications.   Because of many requests received, the Consumers' League of New York has sent its reports to the Department of Economics of the leading universities.   Three of the publications of the National League have been included in the curricula of some of the leading colleges in our country.   Two of the annual reports of the National League have been published as a supplement to the annals of the American Academy of Political and Social Science.

The fundamental idea of the Consumers' League was to arouse a public conscience, with a view to creating a public opinion that would become a dynamic force for good in the community.   We started the movement with zeal and enthusiasm to correct certain specific evils which had been brought to our attention. But not one of that small group of women who started the movement dreamed of the enormous power that they were setting in motion. We educated merchants to see the wisdom of granting vacations. If working girls were to have vacations, where were these vacations to be spent? The vacation houses which have sprung up all over the country, by sea, by lake, by mountain-side, are the answer to this question.

We educated merchants to demand efficiency and skill. If efficiency and skill are demanded in industry, where are the workers to obtain the necessary comfort and seclusion which would give them the rest and re-freshment for the next day's work? Like magic, working girls' hotels have been founded to meet this new need. In New York, the Association to Promote Proper Housing for Girls has made a special study of this problem, inaugurating community clubs for the girls.

While the Consumers' League has been responsible for pioneer work in many directions, it has always been glad to have other organizations formed for the purpose of carrying on any special piece of work. In this way, an influential group of men and women formed the National Child Labour Association, with branches in several states, in order to concentrate on the abolition of child labour. Another group of men and women organized to promote legislation looking towards the furtherance of better labour conditions—the Associa-tion for Labour Legislation. A third group, consisting of well-known captains of industry and labour leaders, coöperated under the name of the Civic Federation, with the view to a better understanding between capital and labour and to further their common interests. We aroused the federations of women's clubs and the woman suffrage organizations to the importance of appointing committees on the industry of women and children, to study local conditions, and to coöperate with the Consumers' League in our work to better these conditions.

It has been left for me to tell the story of the Consumers' League. In looking back over the thirty-six years that have passed since the movement was first started, I am impressed with the entire change of attitude of mind of all the constituents that form the industrial world. I do not claim for the Consumers' League credit for the many remedial agencies organized, or for *all* the welfare legislation enacted; but I do feel that I am not claiming too much in asserting that to the Consumers' League must be paid the tribute of having aroused a dormant public conscience. It has made clear a sense of personal responsibility in the economic world, and it has created and crystallized a public opinion in the community which makes for high standards. Because of this, I feel justified in calling it an epoch-making movement.

CHAPTER VII

LOOKING FORWARD

One who never turned his back but marched breast forward,
Never doubted clouds would break,
Never dreamed, though right were worsted, wrong would triumph,
Held we fall to rise, are baffled to fight better, sleep to wake.

No, at noonday in the bustle of man's work-time
Greet the unseen with a cheer!
Bid him forward, breast and back as either should be,
"Strive and thrive," cry "Speed,—fight on, fare ever
There as here."

—BROWNING.

IN THE previous chapters I have shown how the Consumers' League idea came into being, how it was nurtured, and how it developed and expanded. Has this expansion reached its peak? No movement can stand still; it must either go forwards or go backwards. If it remains static, it is no longer a movement. It would seem wise to determine, first of all, whether there be any reason for the further development of the fundamental principle of the Consumers' League idea. Has the Consumers' League done the work that it set out to do, and is there any special work now to be done which could not just as well be undertaken by some other organization or group of persons? In what way does the Consumers' League differ from the ever-increasingly lengthy list of educational, philanthropic, or social organizations? It seems to me that no other association has awakened the dormant sense of responsibility in the individual as has the Consumers' League, and the quickening of this individual conscience has developed the group conscience. It is only through this group conscience that wrongs can be righted and that industrial conditions can be changed.

If this be true, then the work of the Consumers' League is peculiar to itself and is but in its infancy; its potential power has no limit. Other organizations are created in order to reach a specific goal, whether it be the establishment of a church, a school, a hospital, a community centre, or to accomplish some remedial or welfare work. The goal of the Consumers' League is deeper than this. Primarily, it fosters spiritual growth. It is the affirmative answer to the question, "Am I my brother's keeper?"

As I look back upon the former exploitation of children and of young girls in industry, I am amazed at the progress that has been made in our country within a half century. The problems of child labour, the low wage, and the long working day are still to be wrestled with in certain sections of our country; though, as compared with conditions thirty-five years ago, the standard has been raised. The "truck system" has been abolished; child labour has been lessened; the number of sweatshops has been diminished; the forty-eight-hour week is gradually becoming the standard; the standards of the week-end holiday and of vacations with pay have been established. It cannot be said that there is no more work to be done. There are still many abuses to be righted, still many evils to overcome. But the public has had its dormant conscience aroused and is alert to aid in improving working conditions.

As I review the past and envisage the future, it appears clear to me that the force of the Consumers' League idea is yet to be felt in the economic world. In the solving of industrial problems, there must be a triple alliance. Heretofore, there have been usually but two factors considered—labour and capital. To these there must be added the third—the consumer. The consumer has a wonderful opportunity to influence human relations in industry. When the small store was tended by the owner and by one or two assistants, usually members of the family, this human relationship was not lacking. When the department store replaced the small store, and large armies of clerks were employed, this personal relationship between employer and employee was lost. In the same way, when machinery replaced hand work, and factories grew to enormous proportions, the old personal relationship ceased. Those who tended the machines were considered as part of the machinery and were treated accordingly.

It is only comparatively recently that capital has realized that this former personal relationship must be restored. Not only in order to raise standards of conditions for employees and make their lives less sordid and gray, but also because such personal intercourse is bound to make for better understanding and consequent better workmanship, resulting in greater efficiency.

Many industrial corporations have been experimenting with various plans to secure the point of view of their employees, in order to obtain these results.

One such notable experiment has been made by the Baltimore & Ohio Railroad. This experiment might be said to mark an epoch in industrial progress. This corporation has recognized the trinity of Capital, Labour, and the Public in its effort to bring into harmony the rights of these three factors. What are these rights? Capital has a right to demand a fair return for its investment of money. Labour has a right to demand a fair wage, good working conditions, and a voice in the control of those conditions, in return for its investment of time and strength used in helping to build up the industry. The public or the consumer has the right to demand good service at a reasonable rate in return for its investment in taxes, confidence, and good will, through which it creates the market for the industrial output.

The president of the Baltimore & Ohio Railroad, Mr. Daniel Willard,[1] does not hesitate to express his satisfaction with the plan developed by that company. The plan of coöperation gives equal consideration to capital, labour, and the public. In an address given by Mr. Willard on the occasion of the Golden Jubilee celebration of the city of Garrett, Indiana, in October, 1924, he said:

[1] It is interesting to recall the fact that, at a dinner attended by the members of the Council of the National Institute of Social Sciences, as guests of Mr. Austin Fletcher, in 1921, I had the privilege of sitting next to Mr. Willard. We discussed the Consumers' League movement, and he asked me to send him the League literature. I did so and received a letter from him thanking me for the pamphlets which he found most interesting.

I feel certain that the friendly and sympathetic efforts of both parties will suggest new methods and new practices that will not only make for economy and thereby enable the railroad to pay good wages, and at the same time maintain satisfactory working conditions, but will also contribute towards giving to the public the lower rates for transportation service, which they desire. . . . *First of all, it is our duty . . . to give the public "adequate service at reasonable rates."*

Another notable experiment, but in an entirely different field of industry, has been made by a well-known Boston firm: William Filene's Sons. In this instance, it was also sought to reconcile the divergent points of view of the employer, the employee, and the consumer. In the firm's plan of coöperation a special board of arbitration was formed, consisting of a representative of the management, a representative of the workers, with a third member elected by these two, this third member to represent the public or consumer.

These instances are merely typical of the new trend of thought in modern industry that is gradually making itself felt and becoming with increasing force the accepted standard.

To those interested in economic problems these facts are most encouraging. They are the index fingers that point the way to a better time coming.

To my self-imposed query, "Has the Consumers' League reached its peak?" my answer is: The work of the Consumers' League will never be fully accomplished. It is an educational work which, in its very nature, must be progressive. The League must continue to encourage consumers to throw their weight and power constantly on the side of justice and fairness. Consumers must recognize their own power and, through the force of public opinion, must not only insist upon high standards in industry, on the part of both capital and labour, but must maintain their own rights in regard to good service, free from the exploitation of either of the other two factors. At the risk of repetition, I feel that it cannot be too strongly emphasized that the rights of consumers are to be respected equally with the rights of capitalists and workers.

The consumer is the lever which controls the balancing rod of the two great forces in the industrial world. As the consumer throws the weight of public opinion to the one side or the other, such force is weakened or strengthened accordingly. When a point of issue arises between these two forces, which must of necessity affect the well-being of the public, it is then that the consumers must wield their power and refuse to be victimized. They must insist upon conciliation and arbitration.

The public complains when it is inconvenienced through the deprivation of the necessities of life, as, for instance, coal, milk, transportation, when a conflict of opinion arises between employer and employee. The public complains, but what does the public do? Nothing. The public is supine, it is patient and long-suffering; it waits upon the exhaustion of one side or the other to remedy its condition.

When consumers organize, as capital and labour have organized, their power will be greater than either of the other two forces. The consumer will then be in a position to dictate terms.

Professor Gide has said, "The consumer is king in the economic world." He can be more than king, he can be dictator. This dictator need not be arbitrary, he can be fair-minded and beneficent, coöperating with labour and capital in such manner as to bring about the complete democratization of the economic world.

AUTHOR'S NOTE

Since my manuscript has been in the hands of the publishers, Dr. Edward T. Devine's book on coal has been published. I have been interested to notice that this well-known authority on economics has stressed the point that forms the very cornerstone of the Consumers' League idea.

The American Review Service Press in calling attention to the book, brings out this fact so clearly that I consider that it adds to the force of my own book to quote the following paragraph:

Doctor Devine points out in "Coal"—the Consumers more than any other class must bear the responsibility of settling the coal problem. Consumers must be educated regarding the proper production, marketing, and distribution of coal—Consumers must coöperate to prevent wastes, to minimize accidents in the industry, and maintain peace between operators and miners.

In other words, it's up to us (THE CONSUMERS). And why not? We CONSUMERS pay the bill!

APPENDICES

APPENDIX A

Extracts from the Report of Alice Woodbridge, read at the Meeting of the Working Women's Society, in 1890.

First: We find the hours are often excessive, and employees are not paid for overtime.

Second: We find they work under unwholesome sanitary conditions.

Third: We find numbers of children under age employed for excessive hours, and at work far beyond their strength.

Fourth: We find that long and faithful service does not meet with consideration; on the contrary, service for a certain number of years is a reason for dismissal. It has become the rule in some stores not to keep any one over five years, fearing that the employees may think they have a claim upon the firm, or, in other words, that they will expect to have their salaries raised.

Fifth: The wages, which are low, are often reduced by excessive fines.

Sixth: We find the law requiring seats for saleswomen generally ignored; in a few places, one seat is provided at a counter where fifteen girls are employed; and in one store, seats are provided and saleswomen fined if found sitting.

In all our inquiries in regard to sanitary conditions and long hours of standing and the effect upon the health, the invariable reply is that, after two years, the strongest suffer injury.

APPENDIX B

Statement Issued by the Association Organized in London in 1890

This association is an attempt on the part of persons who are themselves buyers, to make it easier for buyers, who wish to do so, to avoid injustice in their dealings. We recognize that each of us is responsible for the conditions under which work done for us is done, and that the employer is virtually powerless to improve these conditions so long as the customer persists in buying in the cheapest market, regardless of how cheapness is brought about.

But no buyer has time to find out for himself what the conditions actually are under which those things which he purchases are made. He needs a sort of register similar to the list of "fair houses" published by some trade unions. This register should be the result of systematic inquiry, should be easily accessible, should be constantly kept up to date, and should contain the names of those employers only whose workers are proved to be receiving fair payment, and to be working under fair conditions.

To draw up such a register is one of the purposes of the proposed Consumers' League.

We shall appeal to employers to allow inquiry into the conditions of their work people, and we believe there are many who would gladly help to make public the actual conditions in their trade. We shall be ready to include in our list any employer who desires to be placed upon it, and who, after investigation, is found to fulfill the required conditions.

We are well aware that the task before us is a large and difficult one. We are taking it up in no spirit of animosity towards any class, and shall be always anxious to rectify any errors which are shown to us.

Whether we succeed or not in doing any real good will depend upon the number of buyers who show their wish to deal justly by joining themselves to us, and giving their custom to those whose names appear on our lists.

We are asserting, in regard to individual buyers, the principle which has already been asserted in regard to corporate bodies by the London School Board, the London County Council, and many other public bodies, that not the lowest wage, but a fair wage, should be paid. We believe that the great majority of our fellow citizens desire to carry out this principle, if they could but see a way of doing so. To show them such a way is the object of this association.

APPENDIX C

List of Incorporators of The Consumers' League of the City of New York

Maud Nathan (Mrs. Frederick Nathan)
Margaret B. Dewees (Mrs. H. M. Dewees)
Annie Stone
Louise S. Caldwell
Josephine Shaw Lowell

APPENDIX D

List of Officers and of the Advisory Board of the Consumers' League of the City of New York, 1891.

President: Mrs. Charles Russell Lowell
Treasurer: Mrs. Charles A. Spofford
Recording Secretary: Miss Louise Caldwell
Corresponding Secretary: Mrs. Robert V. McKim

Advisory Board

Mrs. Lyman Abbott	Dr. Rosa Welt Straus
Mrs. Mornay Williams	Miss Margaret Finn
Miss Mary E. Vinton	Miss Lenora Smith
Miss Louise Caldwell	Mrs. Charles A. Spofford
Mrs. Charles R. Lowell	

Vice-Presidents

Dr. Mary Putnam Jacobi	Mrs. Edward Lauterbach
Mrs. Frederick Nathan	Mrs. D. M. Stimson
Mrs. Richard Irvin	Mrs. F. C. Barlow
Miss Louise Watson Clarke	Miss F. J. Pomeroy
Mrs. H. Ollesheimer	Miss Annie Stone
Mrs. Helen Campbell	

List of Members of the First Governing Board of the Consumers' League of the City of New York, from the Report Published in 1895.

President: Mrs. Charles Russell Lowell
Treasurer: Miss A. Stone
Recording Secretary: Miss Caldwell
Corresponding Secretary: Miss F. J. Pomeroy

Mrs. George F. Canfield   Miss Edith Minturn
Mrs. H. M. Dewees   Miss S. A. Moller
Mrs. Bolton Hall   Mrs. Frederick Nathan
Mrs. Harmon D. Hull   Mrs. Emmett R. Olcott
Dr. Mary Putnam Jacobi   Miss M. Slade
Mrs. Edward Lauterbach   Mrs. C. A. Spofford
Mrs. Seth Low   Miss H. P. Stokes
Dr. Dorothea Lummis   Mrs. C. W. Watson
Miss Mary Lusk   Mrs. G. C. Wilde

APPENDIX E

Extract from the Message of Governor Theodore Roosevelt, Published in the Report of the Consumers' League of New York, 1898

The development in extent and variety of industries has necessitated legislation in the interest of labour. . . .

At present the enforcement of the law regulating the hours of labour of minors under fourteen years of age and of women employed in mercantile establishments, and the sanitary condition of stores and buildings used for similar purposes in large cities, is left to the Board of Health. If the city government fails to furnish the proper appropriation and appoint the necessary officers to carry out the law, as is at present the case in New York City, it is practically a dead letter. . . .

In various trades the relations between labour and capital have frequently been adjusted to the advantage of both by conferences between intelligent employers and reasonable workingmen. Such mutual understanding is in the highest degree desirable; it promotes industrial peace and general prosperity. Where disturbance exists, and before it has gone too far, the Board of Mediation and Arbitration should seek to secure a fair settlement of the difficulties and a re-establishment of harmonious relations. It should also constantly endeavour to promote the extension of intelligent methods of settlement of labour disputes, so that, through the recognition by each party of the just rights of the other, strikes and lockouts may yield to wiser and more peaceful measures. . . .

In order that the desire of the people, definitely expressed in this wholesome legislation, shall be made effective, I recommend that the enforcement of the entire body of legislation relating to labour be placed under the Board of Factory Inspectors. This would simplify the whole question of labour legislation and place the responsibility for its enforcement where it properly belongs, and would also give the maximum efficiency of service with the minimum cost to the state. With a slight increase in the general force of factory inspectors, this work can be done for the whole state, and the object of the legislation be satisfactorily secured to the people. I recommend that the Legislature provide for additional factory inspectors, so as to bring the total number up to fifty, and also that the Governor be empowered to appoint unsalaried deputies.

Another very important phase of this subject is the sweatshop system, which is practically the conversion of the poorest class of living apartments into unwholesome, pest-creating, and crime-breeding workshops. Laws have been enacted by the Legislature to suppress this vile phase of industrial life in our large cities by prohibiting the use of dwellings for the purposes of manufacture. Although the law is quite explicit, and the intention of the Legislature obvious, great difficulty has been experienced in its effective enforcement. It is everywhere agreed that this tenement-house, or "sweatshop" system is degrading to the unfortunate individuals engaged in it, and to the social and moral life of the community in which it exists. How to enforce the law on this subject has perplexed the statesmen of other countries and states as well as our own.

The most effective and uninquisitive means yet devised for accomplishing this end is that recently adopted by Massachusetts, viz.: providing that buildings used for manufacturing purposes must have a permit or license, such license or permit to be granted only on condition that the appointments of the building fulfill the requirements of the law for manufacturing purposes. These permits or licenses ought to be granted by the Board of Factory Inspectors, who should be held responsible for the proper inspection of the buildings and the enforcement of the law.

There are several reasons why this simple method would be effective. It would at once classify buildings used for manufacturing purposes, as a building so used without a permit would be violating the law. It would prevent much friction, because all requirements of the law would have to be fulfilled before the building was used. This would be a great advantage in the erection of new buildings, as proper conveniences, including accessible fire escapes, guarded elevators, and other appointments would be required and easily furnished when new buildings were being erected or when old ones were being changed for manufacturing purposes. Nor does this involve any radical innovation. It is simply applying the recognized principle upon which Boards of Health now everywhere act in requiring that the plans for erecting new buildings or alterations of old ones must be submitted to the Building and Health Department, and a certificate of approval granted, before the building can be erected, alterations made, or the premises occupied. Legitimate manufacturers will not object to this, because they are desirous of furnishing safe and wholesome appointments for their employees. Only those who desire to evade the law and disregard the common demands of sanitation, domestic decency, and wholesome industrial methods will object, and it is these the law desires to reach.

I submit this to the serious consideration of the Legislature, and suggest that an amendment to the law embodying this idea be adopted, to the end that the uneconomic, unwholesome, and un-American sweat-shop system shall disappear from our industrial life.

APPENDIX F

First Published List of Officers and of the Executive Committee of the National Consumers' League

Officers

President: Mr. John Graham Brooks, 8 Francis Avenue, Cambridge, Mass.

1st Vice-President: Mr. Robert H. Gardiner, 1 Joy Street, Boston, Mass.

2d Vice-President: Mrs. Charles Henrotin, 65 Bellevue Place, Chicago, Illinois.

Treasurer: Mr. John Seely Ward, 1 Broadway, New York City.

Recording Secretary: Miss Watmough, Pelham, Pa.

Corresponding Secretary: Mrs. Florence Kelley, 105 East Twenty-second Street, New York City

Honorary Vice-Presidents

Pres. Arthur T. Hadley, Yale University
Prof. W. J. Ashley, Harvard University
Prof. E. R. A. Seligman, Columbia University
Prof. J. W. Jenks, Cornell University
Prof. H. C. Adams, University of Michigan
Prof. C. R. Henderson, University of Chicago
Prof. S. McCune Lindsay, University of Pennsylvania

Executive Committee

Mrs. Frederick Nathan, 162 West Eighty-sixth Street, New York City

Mrs. V. Simkhovitch, 248 East Thirty-fourth Street, New York City

Miss Helen M. Starr, 103 Cliveden Avenue, Germantown, Pa.

Miss Juliette Wall, 1509 Ridge Avenue, Evanston, Ill.

APPENDIX G

Reports of the State Consumers' Leagues

The following reports of the various State Consumers' Leagues have of necessity been condensed, yet in no instance has any important piece of work been omitted. It has been my endeavour to let each local group tell its own story as far as possible, thus emphasizing the special need of its particular locality. Each league has had its own obstacles to overcome, its own special weaknesses to conquer.

It has been difficult to vary these histories. Each league has necessarily undertaken approximately the same plan of work: investigations, publicity of facts, education of consumers, arousing of public opinion, campaigns for enactment of legislation and law enforcement. Some of the leagues have ceased to function. This does not necessarily mean that the community has lost its interest: it may be that the work has been taken over by official bodies or by other organizations. There has been a noticeable lack of self-seeking on the part of the leaders of the Consumers' League movement. The spirit that has guided and hovered over them all has been one which might well be emulated by every association, educational, philanthropic, or social in character.

In mentioning the names of some of the leaders, there has been no desire on my part to make any invidious distinctions. It has happened that the work of these particular women has been brought to my special attention. It has, therefore, been a pleasure to accord to them the recognition which is their due. There are doubtless many others who are equally deserving of being included in this list of honour, but their work has been of such a character that their identity has been lost. I would like, nevertheless, to pay my tribute to these unknown soldiers without whose staunch and faithful help our industrial battles could not have been won. In the winning of these battles, I am glad to record the valuable coöperation of many merchants and manufacturers. The merchant or manufacturer may be as public-spirited as the social worker, but he is often as much the victim of a pernicious system as is the submerged worker. It cannot be said too often that an indifferent, selfish, exacting public is in reality responsible for evil conditions. Nor must it be forgotten that the "public" is made up of individual units. As Professor Smart well says: "We can all clear up our own little corner of creation." In the clearing up of these little corners, it is significant to find that the work of the Consumers' League has been twofold. It was organized primarily in order to enrich the life of the working girl, whose daily grind seemed unnecessarily monotonous and nerve-racking, and whose outlook on life was gray and narrow. It was undertaken so that she might enjoy the fruits of her labour, experience more deeply the fullness of life. Yet the Consumers' League workers were uplifted from depths of ignorance and selfishness in which they had previously been unwittingly plunged, and they experienced a sense of exaltation and inspiration from the work.

The chairman of an important committee of the National Consumers' League once confided to me that the principles and aims of the League had become for her the solace and religion of her life. The Consumers' League has in reality been even more beneficial to the so-called "idle rich" than to the industrious poor. Understanding and sympathy are prerequisites in order to bring contentment and peace to a world of strife and turmoil.

Dr. Richard Ely of the University of Wisconsin begins his opening chapter on "Studies in the Evolution of Industrial Society" with these words: "The history of ideas is the history of man. Ideas distinguish man from all lower animals, and all that is significant in human history may be traced back to ideas."

The Consumers' League idea—the idea of bringing home to the consumer a sense of responsibility for many of the deplorable and unnecessary evils in industry—

is the revolutionary idea which differentiates the Consumers' League from all other philanthropic, educational, and social organizations.

MAUD NATHAN.

CALIFORNIA

The California Consumers' League was organized in 1902 by a group of women who belonged to the San Francisco Centre of the Civic League, with Mrs. John C. Swift as leader. The decision to form a league was brought about as a result of an address given by the president of the New York City League, Mrs. Frederick Nathan, at the San Francisco Civic Centre. Mrs. Nathan was visiting California as a delegate and speaker at the Biennial Convention of the Federation of Women's Clubs which met that year in Los Angeles. Following the addresses given by her in Los Angeles, Santa Barbara, and San José, groups of women in these cities formed local leagues. In Santa Barbara, the League was sponsored by the Normal School. In Pasadena, it was a group of women who were members of the Shakespeare Club who worked quietly and modestly for ten years for the establishment of the Saturday half holiday, early Christmas closing of shops, and sale of labelled garments. Requests for literature were received at the Headquarters of the National Consumers' League in New York from other parts of California as, for instance: the University of California at Berkeley, San Luis Obispo, Watsonville, Long Beach, and from the Juvenile and Adult Probation Office of Santa Clara County. A committee at the Leland Stanford University was formed to promote the cause of some sort of standardized dress for women, and this committee requested the coöperation of the National Consumers' League. The National League, however, pointed out that it could only coöperate by helping the committee to choose a manufacturer who met the standards of the League. The Los Angeles group of women continued their activities longer than did the San Francisco group. The group of women in San Francisco, however, appreciated the work of the Consumers' League, and at an exposition held in the auditorium of the Civic Centre it awarded a medal of honour and a diploma to the National Consumers' League. This group of Consumers' League disciples was followed by another group which centred about the University of California.

In July, 1909, Mrs. Florence Kelley, the general secretary of the National Consumers' League, addressed a meeting of the Association of Collegiate Alumnæ at the Home Club in Oakland. The women present voted to form a Consumers' League. Mrs. Dane Coolidge was elected temporary president and Miss Elizabeth Herrman temporary secretary. The following November the League was organized at a meeting held at the St. Francis Hotel. It was decided to call it the Bay Cities Consumers' League, as the directors wished to interest all those who resided in the neighbouring towns.

The first president of the Bay Cities Consumers' League was Mr. Fred G. Athearn, Superintendent of Railway Clubs and Welfare Secretary of the Harriman railroads. The vice-president elected was Mr. Harris Weinstock, a well-known merchant of Sacramento, who had the reputation of carrying on his business according to very high standards. Mr. Weinstock had but recently returned from a trip around the world; he had been commissioned by the Governor of California to study labour conditions. The secretary elected was Miss Julia Tolman Lee, student of economics, University of California. A strong board of directors was also elected, which included Professor W. C. Mitchell, Dr. Jessica Peixotto, Reverend Bradford Leavitt, and Reverend E. L. Parsons.

The directors secured the coöperation of college women, who investigated department stores by obtaining positions as welfare secretaries in the stores. They also investigated the street trades of children. The campaign for minimum-wage legislation was a feature of the political progressive movement during the years 1910–15.

In 1912, Mrs. Katharine Phillips Edson became a member of the Bureau of Labour; she realized that it was necessary to raise the standards of conditions for women in industry in the State of California. She got in touch with the National Consumers' League and with the Oregon Consumers' League. Mrs. Edson and her fellow members of the Bureau of Labour framed a bill to present to the California Legislature, along the lines of a similar bill which had been passed by the Oregon Legislature, upon the initiative of the Oregon Consumers' League. This bill provided for the establishment of a minimum wage for women and minors and was passed in 1913. The Industrial Welfare Commission was formed and given the authority to establish from time to time minimum wage standards for various fields of work. The Commission also set standards for hours and conditions of employment of women and minors and prohibited night work in the manufacturing and laundry industries. Moreover, it established one day of rest a week and succeeded in limiting the previous long working day in fish, vegetable, and fruit packing and canning industries by the enforced payments of increased rates after eight hours of work.

The Industrial Welfare Commission endeavoured to secure the observance of its standards by obtaining the coöperation of the heads of industries and by routine inspection of plants, with a view to correcting low standards. When these methods proved unsuccessful, the Commission resorted to legal action for the enforcement of its orders.

From July 1, 1922, to June 30, 1924, the Commission collected more than $20,000 due employees from the enforcement of the minimum wage standards. These sums came from mercantile houses, manufacturers, laundries, hotels, restaurants, fruit, vegetable, and fish canneries, general and professional offices, and unclassified occupations.

Because of the unflagging activity of Mrs. Edson and the Industrial Welfare Commission, the Consumers' League of California did not feel the urge to investigate and consider industrial problems. Gradually, the League ceased its activities, and at the present time all the work that is being done in California to maintain high standards in industry is accomplished by the State Industrial Welfare Commission.

CONNECTICUT

The Consumers' League of Connecticut was organized in 1902, and shortly afterwards formed local leagues in Bridgeport, Hartford, Middletown, Southington, and Waterbury. Later on, leagues were started in New London, Fairfield, Colchester, New Haven, and Stamford.

At the present time, however, all the local leagues have consolidated with the state league. It was considered that better work could be accomplished that way. In the small towns of Connecticut, industrial questions do not come to the fore, as in the larger cities, where there are great industrial centres. The directors of the state league have been drawn from various cities, and the directors' meetings, as well as the Annual League meeting, are held in different parts of the state. In 1907, the Connecticut League was fortunate in being able to secure as general secretary a graduate of Smith College, who had also the degree of Doctor of Philosophy from Yale University, and whose scientific training had been further augmented by a semester at Leipsic University and a season at the American School of Archæology in Athens. Thus Dr. Mary Crowell Welles brought to the work of the League a mind trained in accuracy and an ability to accept all evidence at its real value—in short, a scientific mind.

Under Dr. Welles's able guidance, the League has

made studies of various industries and investigations of actual labour conditions; it has drafted bills for the Legislature and has been responsible for the enactment of twelve statutes since 1909. There has never been a demand for the repeal of any one of the twelve, and the only demands for amendments have come from the Consumers' League itself. This is sufficient proof that the manufacturing and mercantile interests have been satisfied with the results of the League's achievements in regard to legislation. Besides this record, other bills, perhaps to the number of a half dozen, have been presented and passed, through the efforts of other organizations which had secured data from the League, and had been urged by the League to bring about these reforms.

The League's first efforts were directed towards getting existing laws enforced. When it found that the law limiting the hours of women and children in factories and stores was very generally violated, the League appealed to the factory inspector. He maintained that there was nothing in the phraseology of the measure which made it imperative for him to enforce the law. The League pointed out that his office had been created and financed for the sole purpose of carrying out the labour laws. The factory inspector's reply was to the effect that he had enough to do without assuming any responsibility not definitely laid upon him. Therefore, the first bill introduced in the Legislature by the Consumers' League was one placing the responsibility of enforcing the employment law definitely and absolutely upon the Department of Labour.

This resulted in the factory inspector's declaration: "*This* law has teeth in it!" The enforcement of labour laws in Connecticut is very different to-day from what it was fifteen years ago, and it is not too much to say that this result is entirely due to the determined efforts of the League.

In order to bring about reforms through legislation and enforcement of law, public opinion had to be educated, and this was accomplished through the usual channels: published reports, lectures, lantern slides in theatres, posters in public places, exhibits held, and interviews given to reporters, in order to obtain publicity through the newspapers.

To sum up the League's legislative work, it secured a state investigation of the conditions of labour of women employed in factories in 1911, and a state investigation of the conditions of the labour of women employed in stores in 1913; secured the Saturday half holiday for women factory workers and the eight-hour day for factory children; abolished night work for women and children employed in factories and stores; provided for the installation and maintenance of sufficient sanitary toilets for employees of both sexes;[1] secured the proper enforcement of the labour laws protecting women and children; doubled the number of women deputy factory inspectors; drafted a bill and assisted

[1]After the passage of the bill providing for sanitary toilets, some twenty-five manufacturers gathered at the Capitol, on the invitation of the Labour Commissioner, and drew up a very advanced sanitary code on the basis of the bill, putting into the code what the League had felt obliged to omit from it. This code is now used as an interpretation of the law and is what was first introduced the year previously.

in its passage to shorten the hours of employment of women in restaurants, cafés, etc.; took children out of injurious occupations and off dangerous machines;[1] raised the age at which boys are permitted to operate fast-running elevators; regulated the employment of boys in bowling alleys; prohibited the employment of boys under eighteen years of age after ten o'clock at night in the messenger service; secured the enactment of a good and enforceable employment certificate law through the agency of the State Board of Education, in 1911; secured a still more effective one in 1921; and through the same agency secured the extension of the scope of the Trade-school Law, so as to permit the state to organize vocational schools for girls, and afterwards secured the passage of a bill to permit the establishment of vocational guidance as a part of the school system.

The League is at present working for the nine-hour day for women factory workers, and the completion of the eighth grade, for children, when practicable, who wish to leave school under sixteen years of age. It has failed thus far to secure the passage of a minimum wage bill for women workers.

The Connecticut Consumers' League can well be proud of its legislative record, since it accomplished these results notwithstanding much determined opposition and an exhibition of bitterness manifested at first by some of the opponents of the measures.

---

[1]One of the attorneys of the Ætna Insurance Company prepared a pamphlet on "Dangerous Trades for Children," which was of very material help in securing the passage of this bill.

Some manufacturers were sufficiently far-seeing, however, to coöperate with the League in its effort to bring about better industrial conditions through legislation. It was largely through the help of two leading manufacturers: William C. Cheney of Cheney Brothers, and George Landers of Landers, Frary and Clark, that the Senate passed the Fifty-five-hour Week Bill.

The Manufacturers' Association of Connecticut sent a representative to one of the hearings, who spoke in favour of a rest period for women factory workers, from 10 P.M. to 6 A.M. However, there were some manufacturers who evaded the law. For example, there was one firm in New Haven that employed women and girls in polishing and buffing rifle barrels for war contracts. The day shift stopped work at 6P.M. The night shift, composed of approximately seven hundred women and girls, worked from 6 P.M. to 10 P.M. The law did not permit them to work after 10 o'clock at night. So the girls were sent into a neighbouring dance hall, where they ate supper and amused themselves until one minute after midnight. As it was then the next day, they were put at work again until 7 A.M.

The League recognizes that there are five causes of poverty and ill health among labouring people: child labour, lack of training, unsanitary conditions of labour, and the overwork and underpay of wage-earning women and girls. In order to do away with these causes, the policy of the League has been to strike at the root of the evil, endeavouring to secure the coöperation of powerful agencies outside of the League.

Under the auspices of the League, the general secretary made an investigation of international scope of vocational training for children under sixteen years of age, and published a book on the subject which as a book of reference has been widely in demand. The League has also issued some important leaflets in relation to the industrial situation in the state and the progress of the League's work, and has published three pamphlets entitled: "The Department Store Girl and Her Friend in the Five and Ten," "Child Laborers in the Shade Grown Tobacco Industry in Connecticut," "Child Labor Brief."

Professor Henry W. Farnam of the Economics Department of Yale University is first vice-president of the Consumers' League of Connecticut, and has been for many years a valuable member, preparing one of the League's pamphlets, contributing generously to its funds, and offering the hospitality of his home for meetings of the Board of Directors.

It is always easier to get a following for palliative or ameliorative work than to get encouragement for work which is experimental but which strikes at fundamental causes. The Consumers' League work may be slow in its processes, but those who have worked for the cause have found it so fundamental and vital as to impel them to continue in its activities, realizing with Herbert Spencer that, however little comparatively can be done, "we must find it worth while to do that little, so uniting philanthropic energy with philosophic calm."[1]

[1]From Report of president of the New York City League, 1903.

COLORADO: 1903–07

No data of work obtainable.

DELAWARE

The Consumers' League of Delaware developed from the Philanthropic Committee of the Wilmington New Century Club and was organized in April, 1907, and incorporated thirteen years later.

Its first efforts were directed towards raising the standard of conditions in local stores. The Standard of a Fair House was adopted and a White List of stores issued.

Consumers' leagues everywhere did the pioneer work for children in industry, which later on was undertaken by the Child Labour Committee. In Delaware the League, in coöperation with the state factory inspector and the authorities of the public and parochial schools, made provision for night schools for children between the ages of fourteen and sixteen, who could not meet even the low educational requirements of the law at that time. Two years after the League was formed, it secured amendments to the Child Labour Law. In spite of its vigorous protests, however, a provision in the new law permitted children otherwise ineligible for a general working certificate to be employed if "the labour of such child is necessary for the support of itself or to assist in the support of its family."

In order to prevent such permits from being given and also in order to prove how very few children relatively were put to work because of extreme poverty, the League established a scholarship fund for needy children, which it has continued to the present time. The provision is still in the law, but permits are rarely given.

Later, in order to give employment and support to needy families upon whom the Child Labour Law worked a temporary hardship, a committee on the cultivation of vacant lots was appointed by the League. This committee functioned as a part of the League's work for several years, and then became an independent organization, which did valuable work during the war.

The League's early Christmas shopping campaign was so successful that, after ten years' effort, it was no longer needed. The merchants and newspaper editors conducted it themselves. During the first year of the movement, prizes were offered to children for the best scrap-book collections of early Christmas shopping cartoons and advertisements. Six years later, a prize essay contest was conducted, in which one hundred and seven essayists competed.

The Delaware League, as did all its sister leagues, coöperated with the National League in endeavouring to create a demand for the White Label; it held exhibits, from time to time, of labelled goods, and in 1910 had a large exhibit in a store on the main business street in Wilmington.

The League in 1911 introduced into the Legislature a woman's labour bill providing for a ten-hour day, sanitary regulations, and for the guarding of dangerous machinery. The bill passed both houses, with little or no opposition. However, adverse influence was brought to bear on the Governor, and he failed to sign the measure. The opposition centred around the provision for a woman factory inspector at the modest salary of $750 a year, and the granting of power to label as dangerous any piece of machinery not guarded according to certain specifications.

The League, with the view of protecting the interests of consumers as well as producers, started an agitation for the proper protection of foods. In 1914, it directed its efforts towards securing a better milk supply for Wilmington. The League gained much publicity through the fact that one of the most prominent milk dealers threatened to bring suit against the League president. Up to that time, the city's milk had been tested only for butter fats, but the League succeeded in securing bacteriological tests, and a system of more careful handling and distribution.

The League's endeavour to secure a weekly half holiday for workers in stores, as well as in factories, succeeded better among the smaller establishments than among department-store firms. Only one department-store firm yielded to the League's solicitation, yet among grocery stores, markets, men's tailoring establishments, furniture and jewellery stores, business stationers, and miscellaneous stores, the half holiday in summer has become general.

Another result of the League's efforts has been the closing of stores at five or five-thirty in summer. None of the better class stores keeps open of an evening, even during the holiday season.

In 1913, the League had the satisfaction of seeing the Ten-hour Law for women pass, with an amendment, however, which weakened it considerably, allowing for one twelve-hour day a week. Even to secure the passage of this conciliatory measure, the League was obliged to conduct a spectacular campaign, and the victory was largely due to the splendid leadership and untiring efforts of Miss Margaret H. Shearman, who, at two different periods, served the League as president.

For this campaign, too, the League had its first paid secretary, the work previously having been done by volunteers. Again, two years later, the League was forced to conduct a campaign to prevent the repeal of the law it had fought so hard to get enacted, and again it won. Two years afterwards the League secured the passage of amendments to the law, extending its provisions to include women in hotels, restaurants, and offices, and the prohibition of night work in certain establishments.

The League found a great need for an industrial placement bureau in Wilmington and while making an investigation prior to the establishment of the bureau, it discovered that better sanitary conditions were requisite in places of employment. So the following year (1917), the League secured the passage of the present Sanitary Law for Female Workers.

A mothers' pension bill, introduced by another organization, was found to be extremely faulty, and the League was permitted to redraft the measure, whereupon the two organizations coöperated and secured its passage. In 1919, the Delaware League launched a campaign for a minimum wage bill; the measure was defeated, but the attention of the public was drawn to the principle involved.

The League next endeavoured to secure hot lunches in public schools, coöperated with other civic bodies to try to reduce the cost of living in Wilmington, and at the League's suggestion a survey was made of the housing situation, as it affected women employees. It started an agitation for a business girls' hotel, but, owing to business depression, a large number of business women left the city and the situation was thus relieved. As a result of the League's interest, a coöperative association was formed in Wilmington, but did not meet with success.

No association constantly endeavouring to raise the standard of industrial conditions can hope to meet with continuous success; there are always many obstacles to overcome and some defeats to record. It is pleasant, therefore, to be able to relate that the Delaware Consumers' League not only scored a triumphant victory in its campaigns to secure and maintain the Ten-Hour Law for women, but it also was victorious in securing in 1923 amendments to the Child Labour Law which gave further protection to working children. Among the provisions are: an eight-hour day and a forty-eight hour week, the raising of the age from fifteen to sixteen years for certain enumerated dangerous occupations, and requiring street traders to wear badges.

At the same time, through the League's efforts, the Wilmington Board of Education raised the standard of compulsory school attendance from the completion of the fifth grade to that of sixth grade, and a few months later to that of the eighth grade, or the age of sixteen.

The Delaware League has at all times coöperated with the labour commissioner, has endeavoured to improve the administrative policy and to secure the best available inspectors. Because of the meagre salaries provided, the League has helped to secure salary increases.

The League's policy has been to keep in close touch with the various social welfare organizations throughout the state and with the state commissions, and it has joined the recently created Delaware Council of Social Agencies.

THE DISTRICT OF COLUMBIA

The Consumers' League of the District held its first meeting in January, 1912. Mrs. Harvey Wiley was its first president. The League was extremely active for a number of years, counting among its achievements the following:

(1) Enactment in 1916 of the first eight-hour law for women in the East (except in Massachusetts).

(2) Initiation of cost of living inquiry by U. S. Bureau of Labour Statistics, showing necessity for minimum-wage legislation.

(3) Enactment of a minimum-wage law in 1919. This law unhappily was declared unconstitutional by the U. S. Supreme Court, April 9, 1923.

(4) Support with other organizations of the Federal Maternity Bill which became law.

(5) Support with other organizations of improved child labour and compulsory education law for the District, a measure which raised age limit for going to work to fifteen years, required completion of the eighth grade, abolished poverty permits, required vacation certificates from fourteen to sixteen years, badged newsboys for these years.

(6) Came to rescue a number of times of girls' dormitories in Washington, first securing their completion, and then their retention, in order to relieve serious shortage of adequate accommodations for working girls.

(7) Inaugurated early Christmas shopping, Saturday half holiday throughout the year, and early closing of stores.

(8) Gave active support to proposed bills to regulate the packing industry, appearing at the hearings, and giving wide publicity to the need for government control of the monopoly. This activity of the League, initiated by Miss Jessie Haver, League secretary for a number of years, was noted everywhere in the press, and was later carried on by a sub-committee of the National League of Women Voters.

(9) Actively supported bill establishing bureau of women in industry in the Labour Department, a bill which became law.

(10) Directed public attention to the use of young girls as messengers, and urged raising the age limit for

this occupation to twenty-one, and forbidding their work at night.

(No data available for this League since 1920, although it is still in existence.)

GEORGIA: 1904-09

The local interest was in shortening the hours of white women in Atlanta stores. Nothing spectacular ever occurred. It was faithful educational work, but as it was impossible to raise money for national work, or for any considerable amount of free distribution of printed matter, the League was soon disbanded.

ILLINOIS

The Illinois Consumers' League was organized in February, 1897, by the Collegiate Alumnæ of Chicago. A standard was adopted and a provisional constitution drawn up. A permanent organization was effected in November, 1898, at a meeting held in Hull House, and Mrs. Charles Henrotin was elected president.

Besides engaging in the usual work of creating a demand for labelled goods, encouraging early Christmas shopping, securing the Saturday half holiday for store clerks in summer, the League, in 1900, supported the journeymen tailors in their strike against home work and their demand that their employers provide workrooms.

The Illinois League was extremely effective for a number of years in amending and securing adequate enforcement of child labour laws. For these years, the League secretary investigated all children applying for work papers to the Cook County Court, and thus put a stop to false testimony by parents regarding the age of their children. Through the League a helpful relationship was established between public and parochial schools and the Labour Department. At Christmas time, the League was especially vigilant to see that the law was enforced which sent young children home from work at 7 P.M. Young children were also banished from the Chicago stockyards where hundreds had formerly worked under dangerous and brutalizing conditions.

The League, in coöperation with the Women's Trade Union League, aided in instigating the monumental investigation by the United States Department of Commerce and Labour of working conditions of women and children throughout the country. The Illinois League made studies of conditions in department stores (written up in the *Journal of Sociology*), tenement home work, employment of stage children, candy impurities, child labour in glass factories, and the placing of the factory inspection department under civil service.

In 1916, the League was merged with the Juvenile Protective Association. The Illinois Consumers' League felt that while the work of the League was done theoretically from the general assumption of the responsibility of the consumer in its working programme, its efforts had been along the lines indicated by the aims of the Juvenile Protective Association. So a reorganization took place and the merger was accomplished.

In reorganizing, the following general purposes were determined upon:

Shortening hours of labour for women.

Prohibition of night work for women.

Extension and enforcement of child labour laws.

Legislative establishment of a minimum wage.

Endeavour to secure Saturday half holiday and Sunday closing.

INDIANA

During the years 1911–17 the usual League activities were carried on for labelled garments and Saturday half holiday for store clerks in summer. In Indianapolis conditions were reported to be extremely unsatisfactory as to hours and sanitary arrangements. The Indiana League carried on a vigorous campaign to educate the shopping public in regard to the evil practice of returning goods, especially from homes where contagious disease existed.

IOWA: 1902–09

Branches or correspondents reported for several years in Des Moines, Clinton, and Humboldt College. In 1913, a league was reported from Coe College. There are apparently no data regarding activities of any of these branches.

KENTUCKY

In 1900, the General Federation of Women's Clubs met in Milwaukee, Wisconsin, where Mrs. Florence Kelley and the president of the New York Consumers'

League gave addresses on the work of the Consumers'
League. The delegates from the Woman's Club of
Louisville were impressed by the story of the movement, and the following year the Consumers' League
of Kentucky was organized.

The League's first undertaking was to urge the purchase of goods bearing the White Label, and, to this
end, it held an exhibit of "labelled" garments and
endeavoured to get the leading department store firms
to place the labelled underwear on their counters.
Because the label at that time was only placed on the
cheaper grade of garments, it was difficult to get a
large purchasing public to buy them. Four years
later a booklet was widely distributed listing the
prices of labelled garments on sale in Louisville stores.

The Kentucky League was successful in its campaigns
for early Christmas shopping and for a five-thirty
closing hour during five months of the year: January,
February, June, July, and one half of March and
August. The Retail Merchants' Association of Louisville, having heard that the Consumers' League had
one thousand names to a petition for shorter hours,
voluntarily closed their stores at the earlier hour and
also advertised, asking shoppers to do their Christmas
shopping early. In 1907, however, the Association
left the matter to individual firms, so that the closing
hour varied according to the standards of individual
merchants.

Finding that many children who should have been
at school were working in factories and stores, the
League assisted in getting Child Labour and Compul-

sory Education laws passed, securing amendments at later sessions of the Legislature. It coöperated in the enforcement of these laws by working with the truant officers, visiting the homes of the truants and, when necessary, supplying shoes and clothing to enable them to return to school. When advised by the Associated Charities that families of these children were in dire need, the League, through the scholarship fund it had established, was enabled to pay the family a pension in order to permit the children to continue their studies.

In 1910, the League made a survey of women's work in Louisville, covering three thousand cases. Realizing, however, the need for more complete information, it petitioned the Governor to appoint a volunteer commission, empowered to make an official survey. This was done the following year, and the president of the Kentucky League was asked to serve as secretary of the commission. A pamphlet was published showing the results of the survey, and the following year (1912) the Kentucky League secured the passage of the Ten-Hour Law for women, *the only law governing the work of women in the state*. It provided for a ten-hour day, a sixty-hour week, seats for women workers, when they did not interfere with work, and exacted toilets separate from those of men. The bill was not as inclusive and progressive as the League would have liked, but it served as a basis upon which discussions could be carried on between the League officers and employers and employees, as to hours, wages, and working conditions in general.

The League aided in the enforcement of the law, and

also coöperated with merchants and grocers in educating consumers to avoid unreasonable requests for goods to be sent on approval or by special delivery.

The first vocational school in Louisville was established in 1914 through the coöperation of the Kentucky Consumers' League and the Board of Education, after a committee from the Consumers' League had worked for eight months acquiring information and selecting a proper instructor. The Consumers' League paid the necessary $2,000 for the salary of the trade teacher. Only those children in greatest need of vocational training were admitted. The experiment was so successful that the Board of Education took over the school the following year. For seven years, however, the League continued to contribute some financial assistance. To show how popular the school became, the attendance grew in ten years from 32 children in 1914 to 1,194 students in 1924, including those who attended, not only the day school, but the afternoon continuation school and the night school. Vocational work having been undertaken two years later (1916) in Mayesville, Kentucky, the Consumers' League contributed seventy-five dollars to the cause. In 1916, the League contributed $400 and, in coöperation with the Board of Education, conducted a vacation school.

The Commissioner of Agriculture, Labour, and Statistics invited the Consumers' League to send a representative to serve on the Advisory Board in order to assist the woman labour inspector to enforce the State Child Labour and Ten-Hour laws. The Consumers' League was instrumental in securing the opening of the first office for the department of labour and assisted in organizing the department's first records. The chairman of the Industrial Committee of the League visited factories and took children out of street trades, while another member of the League kept the records of work done, filed all prosecutions, as well as noted the cases requiring financial aid, and helped to secure the sums needed.

During the years of the World War, the president of the League represented Kentucky on the Committee of Women in Industry, Council of National Defense, where standards for women workers were recommended to government departments and were adopted. Through the information received from the Washington conferences of this committee, work was facilitated throughout the entire state. The League president was also the representative of women employees on the War Labour Community Board for Kentucky.

Owing to the fact that the Secretary of War, the Honourable Newton D. Baker, was also the president of the National Consumers' League, it can readily be seen that suggestions made by the officers of the Kentucky Consumers' League were usually acted upon favourably and maintained during the period of the war.

The Minimum Wage Commission bill prepared by the Kentucky Consumers' League was presented at two sessions of the Legislature, in 1920 and 1922, and notwithstanding the help rendered the League by Miss Jeannette Rankin, who spent a month speaking in favour of the bills and lobbying for them, they failed to pass. In 1921, the League assisted to its utmost the Woman's Bureau which was making a survey of hours, wages, and working conditions of working women in Kentucky. The report made by the Woman's Bureau of the low wages paid to Kentucky working women was used largely in the minimum wage campaign of 1922, but without avail.

The League prepared a bill for the reorganization of the State Labour Department, for presentation to the 1924 General Assembly. The object of the measure was to secure better trained labour inspectors by Civil Service examination, a chief labour inspector, higher salaries, permanent records, the printing of educational pamphlets on industrial health, safety devices, and sanitation so that working conditions might be improved through education. This bill, approved by both labour representatives and employers, was passed unanimously. Since then the League has been coöperating with the Labour Department in collecting Civil Service material. An industrial sanitation code is at present being prepared by the League, adapted from the standards of the United States Public Health Service and the codes of other states as a reference for voluntary acceptance by employers.

Mrs. R. P. Halleck, who has been the able and devoted president of the League since its inception, has been largely responsible for much of the success of its undertakings. No history of any great movement can be complete without touching upon the personal side, suggesting the intense thought given, the energy expended, the sacrifices made, by those who have sponsored the movement from the beginning.

LOUISIANA

In 1915, Miss Jean Gordon, formerly factory inspector of New Orleans, was appointed Consumers'
League secretary for the Southern States. She was
also secretary of the Louisiana State Commission for
the Investigation of the Condition of Working Women
and Children appointed by Governor Hall in 1914.
This commission was created at the instigation of
Miss Gordon. It made an investigation of wages paid
to women and girls in New Orleans. The report
covered thirty-four establishments and showed that
wages were below the level of subsistence.

Miss Gordon's work for child labourers bore such
fruit that, when photographs of working children of
the South were displayed at the National Conference
of Charities and Correction in Memphis, those alone
from New Orleans showed children as large in stature
as in the same occupations in the North or in Western
states.

The League concerned itself with conditions in stores
and endeavoured to bring pressure on firms to open at
8.30 A. M. instead of at 8 o'clock. The League was
active in endeavouring to create a demand for labelled
garments; it also conducted an early Christmas shopping campaign and succeeded in getting all first-class
stores to close at 6 P. M. up to Christmas Day.

The Christmas Savings Bank clubs were appealed to,
and the directors consented to make payments the
following year (1917) during the first week in December
instead of waiting until December 15th. The bank

directors agreed to this most eagerly, so as to remove one of the obstacles to early Christmas shopping. All the students of the H. Sophie Newcomb College joined the Louisiana Consumers' League in observing Child Labour Day. A branch of the Consumers' League had been organized at the college in 1912.

The Louisiana League is still in existence, but all efforts to obtain reports of recent activities have been unsuccessful.

MAINE

During the years 1904-13 a league existed in Maine, but apparently sent no reports of its work to the National Consumers' League.

MARYLAND

The Maryland Consumers' League was organized at a meeting held at the Arundel Club in Baltimore, in 1900, after an address given by the president of the New York City League

Some members of the philanthropic section of the Woman's Club of Roland Park at once formed a committee and undertook to secure the coöperation of Baltimore merchants in an endeavour to get Consumers' League labelled garments into the stores. A list of the garments so labelled with the announcement as to where they could be purchased was prepared, printed, and distributed.

In 1902, the Consumers' League idea was brought to the attention of the Maryland State Federation of Women's Clubs, and a committee was appointed to consider the advisability of organizing a state consumers' league. This was accomplished the following year.

Until March 8, 1918, when the Council of the National Consumers' League decided to abandon the label and to use other methods in order to raise standards in factories, the Maryland League conscientiously and consistently pushed the demand for labelled garments among the women of the state. It succeeded in getting seventeen Baltimore merchants to carry labelled goods. Not only were these firms progressive in this particular, but the majority of them responded favourably to other requests of the League for improved conditions in stores, with the result that seats were provided behind counters, separate lunch and dressing rooms were arranged, the Saturday half holiday granted, and later on, the whole day during July and August, and a shorter working day was inaugurated for the summer months.

The Maryland League had a powerful ally in His Eminence, Cardinal Gibbons, who was one of the League's honorary vice-presidents; he delivered more than one sermon from the pulpit of the Cathedral, calling attention to the work of the League and the necessity to support it. The Maryland League also had the coöperation of Dr. Jacob Hollander and other professors of Johns Hopkins University, and for several years, beginning with 1911, the League claimed as its president Hon. Charles J. Bonaparte, who was the chief supporter of minimum-wage legislation.

The Maryland League is justified in claiming that the passage of the Child Labour and School Attendance laws and other laws of a similar character was largely due to the systematic educational efforts in which the League engaged for many years.   In 1906, the legislative campaign to restrict child labour was conducted and the bill was passed.

The Russell Sage Foundation appreciated the valuable work undertaken by the Maryland League in making a special investigation of conditions surrounding the working women of Baltimore and helped to finance the illustrated report which was published in 1910 in book form under the title "Saleswomen in Mercantile Stores," by Elizabeth B. Butler.

It was not until 1912 that the Maryland League introduced into the Legislature a bill limiting the hours of working women in certain industries throughout the state to ten in one day.   After a thorough investigation of existing conditions, it carried on a vigorous educational campaign; it won a great triumph in securing the passage of the Ten-Hour Law in mechanical, mercantile, manufacturing, baking, and laundering establishments.

Under the provisions of the law, a bureau was created for its administration and the League was asked to select the administrator.   Miss Sarah Martín was chosen, and she was given two inspectors.   As the League believed in a fair wage, it helped to finance the bureau, which was inadequately financed by the state.

In January, 1915, an amendment was added to the League constitution, "providing that the League shall have a council of not less than twenty-five members to conduct all the business of the League and have power to add to its members at any time." This insured awakening and sustaining the interest of a larger group of citizens.

The League started in 1916 a welfare department to improve conditions in regard to the leisure hours of working girls. Each store was assigned to a committee of League workers who were able to deal sympathetically with the industrial girl and her many problems. It was especially the new employee or the stranger in the city, away from her home town and associates, who appreciated the efforts of the League workers. This particular branch of the Maryland League's work was continued for four years.

The League had a booth at the "Made in Baltimore" Exposition at the Fifth Regiment Armoury, September, 1916, showing a picturesque contrast between conditions in a Baltimore factory which was using the Consumers' League label and those in a sweatshop from which an unlabelled garment might have come.

As county merchants were permitted to employ women for twelve hours on six consecutive days before Christmas, besides on every Saturday throughout the year, "Shop Early" cards were printed and widely distributed, especially in rural districts.

In 1917, an investigation was made into the vacation and early closing policies of the various mercantile establishments, and a bulletin was issued asking the shopping public to make purchases at the stores where conditions were best for the workers.

During the period of the war, the Maryland League coöperated closely with the Committee on Women in

Industry of the Women's Section of the Maryland Council of Defense, its executive secretary becoming also the executive secretary of the Committee. Information was collected for the War Department in reference to unemployment in the needle trades; reports were also secured from forty-two industrial plants, with a view to rendering aid to the Federal Director of Employment in Maryland. Investigations were carried on in regard to the new occupations for women which developed as a result of the war; statistics were gathered and ways of improving conditions were considered.

The League worked with the Community Service Organization of Roland Park in establishing a community kitchen, where work could be carried on with greater facility and under better conditions than under the individual housework system.

The League's Standard of a Fair House was published in 1918, and before the leaflet was sent to the printer, it was submitted for consideration to eight leading mercantile firms, all of whom gave it their unqualified approval.
The Maryland Consumers' League points out that many of the Baltimore firms have now of their own initiative adopted the standard upheld by the League in its early days, and many firms who at that time lagged behind in progressive management have now reached the goal of the progressive ones of former times. Thus we again have proof of the good results from educating public opinion.

In 1920, the League for the third time brought a bill before the Legislature for a minimum-wage commission for women and minors. Notwithstanding the vigorous campaign conducted, and the fact that the League had the coöperation of many business and professional men and women, not only in Baltimore, but from states in which the minimum-wage laws were already in operation, and that it had the active support of speakers of national reputation, the bill was unfavourably reported by the Senate Committee and failed to pass.

In an investigation made to determine the actual cost of living of working girls, 160 students of Goucher College coöperated by filling out blanks to show the cost for the average college girl in regard to items concerning the care of health.

The Maryland League has aided in raising scholarship funds for working girls to attend the Bryn Mawr Summer School, and has enabled four working girls to attend Johns Hopkins Summer School.

Thus, it can be readily seen that the Maryland Consumers' League has become a real force in the community and has earned the respect and consideration, not only of those who constantly work to further the community's welfare, but also of employers of labour, who, though realizing the existence of certain evil conditions, have felt powerless to overcome them, because of the relentless and terrible world grind of competition.

MASSACHUSETTS

In 1897, a meeting was arranged by Dr. John Graham Brooks and held in the Y.M.C.A. Hall, on Boylston

Street, Boston, at which the president of the New York City Consumers' League was asked to give the principal address. She spoke on the aims and principles of the League and told of the work already accomplished by the New York League.

Less than a year later, the Consumers' League of Massachusetts held its first public meeting, adopted a constitution, elected its officers, and formed a Committee on Label.[1]

As early as 1898, the Massachusetts League engaged as an investigator of Boston stores, J. McKenzie King, who in 1924 was Premier of Canada. It was due to the publication of Mr. King's pamphlet on hours of work in stores that a bill was introduced in the state legislature by the Federal Labour Union extending the Fifty-eight Hour Law, already protecting textile workers, to women and minors in mercantile establishments. The following year some of the large department-store firms of Boston initiated the eight-hour day.

After hours had been shortened, the League found that conditions in the retail establishments of Boston were better than they had been in New York when the League was organized; therefore, it bent its efforts towards securing better conditions of production of the articles sold over the counters of the stores. It was, therefore, through pressure exerted by the officers of the Massachusetts League that the National Con-

---

[1] The committee on organization consisted of Mrs. C. G. Ames, Mrs. Schlesinger, Mrs. Kehew, Mrs. Deland, Mrs. Staigg, Mrs. Davis R. Dewey, Miss Lucia T. Ames, Miss Warren, Miss Rose Lamb, Mr. Brooks, Mr. R. A. Woods, Mr. John O'Sullivan, Mr. Robert Ely.

sumers' League took up the work of endeavouring to abolish the sweatshop.

It was decided to begin with women's white underwear, since the needle trades were the notoriously sweated ones, and an appeal could be made to women throughout the country to create a demand for underwear made in high standard factories. A label was designed by one of the partners of the George Frost Co. (manufacturers of Velvet Grip Hose Supporters, one of the first firms to use the White Label of the Consumers' League), and slowly one manufacturer after another was prevailed upon to use this label on all the output. It was only after a thorough investigation had been made, including inspection of factory, examination of the records of state factory inspector, and interviews with employers and employees, that a contract was signed and the label awarded. Labels were given only to those manufacturers who had light, sanitary workrooms, who had all their product made on the premises, and gave none out to be made under contract; who demanded no overtime of workers, employed no children under sixteen years of age, and conformed in all respects to the state factory laws. Later on, another clause was added "that when a strike occurs and arbitration is refused by employers, the contract is automatically cancelled." In 1916, there were sixty-eight factories using the White Label of the National Consumers' League. It was evidently considered of commercial value, for a New York manufacturer was found using it illegally, and the National Consumers' League was obliged to bring suit.

The Massachusetts League was always in the vanguard, creating the demand for labelled garments, and upholding the National League in its work in this direction. It aided in inspection of factories by donating the services of its executive secretary, Miss Mary C. Wiggin, who investigated and reinspected many of the Massachusetts factories. Because of her intelligent assistance and her devotion to this branch of the work, she was appointed by the president of the National League, chairman of the Committee on Label.

The Massachusetts League, in coöperation with other organizations, brought about many industrial reforms. It helped to secure shorter hours of work for women and children, reducing them to fifty-eight hours a week and ten hours a day, then later to fifty-four hours a week, and finally to forty-eight hours a week and eight hours a day.

It procured protection for minors from dangerous trades and the prohibition of the employment of children under fourteen on the stage. It assisted in securing changes of administration of labour laws, by transferring the supervision from the District Police to the present unified system of the State Department of Labour and Industries.

In 1908, the Massachusetts Consumers' League formed as a sub-committee, a Joint Child Labour Committee in order to restrict child labour; the following year seven members of the League's Board of Directors formed the nucleus of the Executive Committee of the new organization: the Massachusetts Child Labour Committee. In 1914, the Massachusetts

League was incorporated. During that year the League helped to form a joint committee on Industrial Conditions for Women and Children in Massachusetts. This was done to forestall any move which might be made to set aside labour laws during the war. The Committee is still doing active work to-day, fourteen organizations being represented besides sixteen individuals. The Massachusetts League, through this agency, did valuable service in the community, and its advice was constantly sought in dealing with industrial problems. Through its committees on food it gained the coöperation of large groups of men and women who stimulated the Boards of Health throughout the state to action.

At the instigation of the Women's Trade Union and the Consumers' League, a Minimum-Wage Commission, in 1918, was empowered to fix the minimum wage for various trades. Representatives of employers in the industry, employees, and the public served on the Commission. The Commission has no authority, however, to compel manufacturers to pay this minimum wage, it is only empowered to publish the names of those who refused to comply with the standard fixed.

While this form of minimum-wage legislation was not deemed sufficiently drastic at first, it has stood the test of constitutionality before the Supreme Court, so that other states are now introducing legislation based on the Massachusetts plan. The Massachusetts Supreme Court rendered a decision recently that newspaper editors may not be compelled to publish the names of recalcitrant firms, but it reaffirmed the validity of the measure on other points. All the leading papers but one in Boston therefore continued to accept the notices for publication.

The Massachusetts League kept up its early Christmas shopping and its early closing campaigns until they were taken over by the retail firms, who spread the propaganda themselves among their clientèle. It published White Lists of tailors who had all their garments made on the premises, of bakeries which were found to be sanitary and were not in cellars, and of restaurants where employees worked under good conditions.

The League published from time to time bulletins on: "The Minimum Wage," "The Administration of Law," "Post Office Service," "Conditions in Food Establishments," "Fire Risks in Industrial Establishments," and "Unemployment." The League was constantly called upon to furnish speakers for meetings and clubs throughout the state.

The League in 1915 provided relief for impoverished custom tailors by opening workrooms where 2,500 dress skirts and 45 suits were made and sent to Belgian refugees.

The Massachusetts League has been preëminent in its close contact with the State Labour Department. It has led in the movement to keep the Department out of politics, and it has had measures amended and methods corrected until to-day Massachusetts has the reputation of having the best system of law enforcement in the country.

Miss Mary C. Wiggin has been for many years the able executive secretary of the Massachusetts League.

MICHIGAN

From 1900–09 there were four branches of this league more or less active, in Detroit, Ann Arbor, Grand Rapids, and Jackson. During the first year, the League introduced a bill providing for a woman factory inspector. By the end of the second year, two women inspectors were appointed. The League was also effective in Grand Rapids and in Detroit in introducing labelled goods, and in improving shopping habits. It conducted a campaign for early Christmas shopping and to obtain a half holiday in summer for store clerks, etc. Many educational meetings were held throughout these centres to discuss League principles, and much literature distributed. In 1905, the Child Labour Law was amended through the League's efforts.

MISSOURI

The Consumers' League of Missouri has for more than twenty years upheld the traditions of the National League. The League, through its efforts, succeeded in securing the passage of the law restricting the working day for women to nine hours and aided in its enforcement when it discovered violations; it also aided very materially in securing the enactment and enforcement of the bill to restrict the labour of children to eight hours a day and prohibiting their working under fourteen years of age. It assisted in getting the Juvenile Court Bill and the Mother's Pension Bill passed. Members of the Social Legislation Commission representing various organizations active in the legis-

lative campaign agreed that these laws could not have
been passed but for the effective work of the Consumers'
League. The League found that the law required no
inspection of factories in cities of less than 10,000
population, and it has been endeavouring to have the
inspection extended to cover rural towns where many
factories were located after the passage of the law
requiring inspection of city factories. The League
conducted training classes in factory inspection, and
the attendants were afterwards made deputy inspectors.
The League, in its constant endeavours to protect
workers, discovered that the new building code of
St. Louis omitted to require that exits to fire escapes
be constructed of fireproof material. No other organization or individual had noticed this serious omission.
The League drew up a new ordinance, requiring outside
iron fire escapes, which was passed, thus helping to
protect thousands of factory workers.

The Consumers' League of Missouri was the first
agency to bring to the attention of employers and
employees the importance of definite training in
salesmanship in order that employers might demand
higher standards of efficiency and employees obtain
higher wages. The League had a booth at the Household Show held at the Coliseum. It held, from time to
time, exhibits of labelled garments from St. Louis
stores, publishing the names of the firms where these
garments could be purchased. Side by side with the
labelled underwear were the graphic and interesting
exhibits of the National Consumers' League, showing
articles made in sweatshops and tenement rooms.

The League worked unceasingly to secure a half holiday on Saturdays during the summer months, and succeeded in getting four of the principal department stores to close at 1 P. M. on Saturdays during July and August.

The Consumers' League of Missouri, through its active Food Committee and in coöperation with the State Food Inspector, conducted widespread inspections of food shops, including six hundred bakeries. In order to raise the standard of cleanliness, light, and ventilation, it issued the following White List certificates to those which were good enough to be graded 95 per cent. or above (100 per cent. being considered perfect):

We are on the
White List
of the
Consumers' League
Issued to———

These certificates were displayed in the shops where they were awarded, and members were asked to deal only with those butchers, bakers, grocers, and confectioners who could show them. The League conducted this campaign in coöperation with the State Food and Drugs Department.

The League also conducted a fly-exterminating campaign, working through schools in coöperation with the Health Department. The League distributed 70,000 fly swatters in the public schools, together with pamphlets explaining the importance of exterminating flies.

The Missouri League conducted a vigorous Christmas

"Shop Early" campaign; the merchants coöperating by enclosing early shopping notices with the bills sent out to customers December 1st. In 1914, the Associated Retailers of St. Louis carried on their own Christmas "Shop Early" campaign, along the same lines formerly pursued by the Consumers' League.

The Consumers' League of Missouri has always sought the coöperation of other bodies in endeavouring to raise industrial standards, and has shown a willingness to participate in bringing about better civic conditions. The League has been represented on the committee of the Mayor's Conference, in St. Louis, the Central Council of Social Agencies, the Social Service Conference, and the Advisory Committee to the Mullanphy Board. The League helped in the preparation of ordinances to better conditions in police courts and dance halls.

At the time of the World War, when the General Secretary of the National Consumers' League was a member of the Board of Control of Labour Standards for Factories making uniforms, the Secretary of the Missouri League received an official commission to inspect local factories making army supplies. It was thus possible to correct promptly any undesirable conditions. Because of the wide experience of the secretary of the Missouri League, she was asked by the War Work Council of the National Young Women's Christian Association to look into the welfare work undertaken for women munition workers in France. This was done at the request of the French Government.

The Food Committee of the League did specially

valuable work during the war. It was commended for its systematic and effective work in conservation. It established community kitchens for selling cooked foods at cost, to be eaten either at the kitchens or to be taken home in containers; it also inaugurated a wagon service for near-by factories and conducted the feeding of undernourished school children. The kitchens were afterwards taken over by the St. Louis Chapter of the American Red Cross as part of their public health work. When the National Board of the Young Women's Christian Association decided to establish an industrial service centre for employed girls and later determined to make a survey of conditions affecting working women in St. Louis, its field worker consulted the secretary of the Consumers' League, who was glad to coöperate in accomplishing these tasks.

The Missouri Consumers' League was able to render assistance to the Red Cross Home Service Department in regard to cases in which returned soldiers were given industrial positions. Not only did municipal and state organizations turn to the League for advice and help, but welfare workers in factories also came to the League office with requests for suggestions in developing plans for working girls. The indefatigable and efficient secretary, Mrs. Harry January, has been associated with the League since its inception, and a large share of the progress of its work is due to her untiring zeal.

NEW JERSEY

The New Jersey Consumers' League has accomplished some remarkable achievements. Before it was organized, in March, 1901, there was little or no legislation regulating the industry of women and children. The only two laws which affected working women were practically dead letters. The provision requiring seats behind counters in stores had no penalty attached for violation; consequently, the law was not observed. The Factory Act limiting the hours of women working in factories to fifty-five a week was not enforced. Only in one instance was its enforcement attempted; the matter was contested but the case was never brought to trial.

Under the law existing at that time, boys of twelve and girls of thirteen years of age were permitted to work all night in glass factories. One little child of seven was so exhausted after working all night in one of these factories, that he stopped on his way home, fell asleep near the railroad tracks, and was killed by a passing train.

Children under legal age were able to secure working certificates from the chief factory inspector, if the parents claimed to be in need of this extra income and wished to put the children at work. No educational qualification was required in order to obtain the working certificate. There was so little inspection by the State Factory Department that its function was looked upon as a farce.

The New Jersey Consumers' League started at once to make an investigation in regard to hours of work. The investigators found women and children working in factories from 7 A. M. to 9 P. M. There was no limit to the working hours of women in any industry before the passage of the Ten-Hour Law (which granted exemption for the two weeks before Christmas). At the time that the project to organize a consumers' league was being considered, the mercantile establishment in Newark which had the best reputation as to conditions of work was advertising: "We keep open fourteen hours on Saturday."

When the stores had the greatest crowds and the work was the most exhausting, hours were unlimited; young children as well as women were often found working until after midnight. The League's first action which brought it into public notice was its attack on the inefficiency of the Factory Department. Articles were published in newspapers and magazines, and a petition was sent to Governor Voorhees asking him to appoint a woman factory inspector.

It took nearly four years of persistent effort to educate public opinion and get conditions remedied. Finally, in 1904, the old Factory Department went out of existence and was succeeded by a new Labour Department, supervised by a Labour Commissioner.

The Commissioner of Labour was sympathetic towards every effort of the Consumers' League to improve conditions for women and children. The Labour Department became a model for every state in the Union.

In order to secure better protection for children in industry, the Consumers' League called a meeting of all organizations interested in their welfare, the outcome of which was the formation of the Children's Protective Alliance, which later on developed into the Child Labour Committee.

Every bill for improving conditions of children in industry up to the year 1915 was introduced by these allied organizations, and several bills were enacted into laws through their efforts, with the result of restricting considerably the work of children.

Twenty-two years after the League was organized, a different picture is presented in regard to the industrial field. No manufacturing or mercantile establishment, no bakery, laundry, or restaurant is permitted to employ women longer than ten hours a day or fifty-four hours a week, with no exemption at the Christmas holiday season. Canneries, however, are not included in the law. In the Department of Labour, three women inspectors really inspect, and at the head of the Bureau of Safety a woman functions. Sanitary laws have been enforced, seats have been placed behind counters in stores, and a penalty exacted for violation of this measure; night work has been prohibited in factories and laundries after 10 P. M. and before 6 A. M.

Progressive employers, through pressure brought by public opinion, aroused by the League, have granted a Saturday half holiday to their employees in summer, and many stores have closed all day Saturday during July and August.

The New Jersey League brought to the attention of the Commissioner of Labour the growing evil of home work, which seemed to be getting more and more extensive. Under the supervision of one of the deputy commissioners, an investigation was made and the deputy, in a letter to the president of the League, gave entire credit to the League for having proved the need of the investigation.

The League conducted a campaign for the enactment of a minimum-wage commission law, which, in 1923, passed the Assembly, but was lost in the Senate.

During the war the president of the New Jersey League was appointed chairman of the Committee on Industry for the National Council of Defense of the State of New Jersey. She was also made assistant commissioner for New Jersey of the Federal Employment Service; this required the cöoperation of the Consumers' League, as the commissioner, Colonel Bryant, also Commissioner of Labour, permitted no drive for workers in industrial plants until these plants had been inspected and met the standards issued by the United States Department of Labour.

Mrs. G. W. B. Cushing has been president of the Consumers' League of New Jersey since its organization. Through her zeal and her untiring efforts, the League has been one of the great moral and civic forces of the state. She also served for many years as recording secretary of the National Consumers' League and is at present one of its vice-presidents.

The maxim adopted by the New Jersey League is well worthy of consideration: "Social justice is the best safeguard against social disorder."

NEW YORK STATE

Plans for forming the Consumers' League of New York State were informally discussed in January, 1898, but it was not until February 24, 1900, that the League was organized, a constitution adopted, and officers elected. This first meeting was held at the Friendly Aid Settlement House, 248 East 34th St., Mrs. Vladimir Simkhovitch presiding. Mrs. Frederick Nathan was asked to be the first president of this newly formed league, but as she was already president of the New York City League, she declined the honour. However, she was elected vice-president, and served as acting president until 1903, when Miss Sadie American was elected to the office. The first secretary was Miss Rowena Buell, and the first treasurer, Miss Florence Colgate.

At the meeting held in February, 1900, there were delegates from Utica, Syracuse, Yonkers, Flushing, Ithaca, and New York. It was reported that leagues were in the process of being formed in Rochester and Brockport. In the constitution it was stated that the special object of the New York State League was to bind together for effective concerted action all leagues to be formed in the state.

The Brooklyn Consumers' League had been organized in 1895 by Mrs. Ruth Huntington Sessions, a daughter of Bishop Huntington. She was the first president of the League and continued in office until she gave up her residence in Brooklyn, and moved to Massachusetts. Mrs. Lillian W. Betts succeeded her and remained president of the League until 1907, when it was decided to make the Brooklyn League an auxiliary branch of the New York City League, the president and one delegate attending the New York City board meetings. The Brooklyn League has done valiant work ever since it was first organized. After

it united with the New York City League, it continued
under the able leadership of its chairman, Mrs. Stephen
Loines, to conduct investigations, hold exhibits, assist
the Brooklyn Health Department in its work of issuing
working certificates to children, and was instrumental
in bringing about changes in the school system in connection with this branch of work. The League co-
operated in early Christmas shopping campaigns, legislative work, and enforcement of labour laws, and also
published a handbook of the state labour laws. One of
the most important pieces of work undertaken by the
League was an investigation of tenement homes where
manufacturing was carried on. At present, its principal
work consists in providing a scholarship for a Brooklyn
girl for the Bryn Mawr Summer School of Industrial
Workers.

During the years of 1907–08 the New York State
Consumers' League, under the leadership of Mrs.
Robert McVickar, engaged Dr. Mary Taylor Bissell, a
sister of President Taylor of Vassar College, as field
secretary. She travelled throughout the state organizing local leagues in various centres. Among
those organized were the leagues of Mt. Vernon, Hud-
son, Albany, Schenectady, Fayetteville, Olean, Au-
burn, Elmira, Kingston, Poughkeepsie, Watertown,
and Buffalo.

Later on, there were many school leagues organized,
as for example: the Albany College for Teachers, St.
Agnes School, Albany; Packer Collegiate Institute,
Brooklyn; Mechanics' Institute, Rochester; Syracuse

University, Solvay High School, Syracuse; and Vassar College, Poughkeepsie.

Many of these local branches were only active when aroused by speakers from New York or by the field secretary, Doctor Bissell. The Buffalo League was the strongest, having secured a large membership which enabled it to have an office and an executive secretary. The Buffalo Consumers' League did good work in investigating conditions and in working with girls engaged in industry. The League participated actively in all state investigations and legislative work. Miss Sarah L. Truscott was president for a number of years.

In Rochester, the League had the active coöperation of the Women's Educational and Industrial Union.

Under the leadership of Miss Caroline A. Whipple, and later under Mrs. Campbell Macmillan, the Schenectady Consumers' League did admirable work. It could always be counted upon to assist with state investigations and to provide delegates for legislative hearings at Albany. The League succeeded in getting the mercantile establishments to grant a Saturday half holiday in summer to employees.

In Utica, Miss Lucy Carlile Watson has been the guiding spirit from its inception. In the spring of 1900 the president of the New York City League was asked to address a mass meeting in order to arouse interest in the newly formed League. The state factory inspector, whose home was in Utica, was among her auditors. He was surprised to learn that Mrs. Nathan had that afternoon been inspecting some of the tenement homes where clothing was being made in unlicensed houses. After the meeting the factory inspector met Mrs. Nathan and the officers of the local league and promised his hearty coöperation. For a number of years Mrs. J. T. A. Doolittle was president of the Utica League, which has always responded effectively to the demands of the State League.

Miss Emma Beard organized the League of Fayette-ville, and from the very beginning of the work she has been most assiduous in striving to accomplish the aims of the League. For many years she was the president of the New York State League, and her zeal and enthusiasm have never lagged.

The Syracuse Consumers' League has had for many years the unflagging interest and enthusiastic leadership of Mrs. Horace A. Eaton. It has taken an active part in endeavouring to restrict child labour. It conducted a successful campaign against permitting very young children to peddle newspapers in the streets. An accident which crippled a small newsboy was the means of arousing the public conscience through a mass meeting. One of the results was that the League secured the appointment of a special attendance officer on the school board, whose entire time was given to the enforcement of the newsboy law. It was learned that the crippled boy of fourteen had, according to his mother's statements, scarcely spent a night at home since he had been seven years of age. He had passed his nights in the alleys waiting for the early morning edition of the newspapers. The Syracuse League also conducted campaigns to bring about the Saturday half holiday in summer and the six o'clock closing of stores. The League has been a pillar of strength to the State Consumers' League and Mrs. Eaton is at the present time the corresponding secretary of the New York League.

For about eight years the New York State headquarters were in Syracuse. The League constantly coöperated with other state associations in its legislative work. It kept in touch with the Women's Federation of Clubs, the Parents' and Teachers' Association, the League of Women Voters, and the Women's Christian Temperance Union. The League also took advantage of state fairs in order to spread its propaganda. Two state-wide wage studies were conducted with special investigators in charge.

In 1920 the State League coöperated with the Joint Legislative conference, working for minimum wage legislation and for the eight-hour working day for women. Representatives attended hearings on the recodification of the labour law and worked to attain the Bureau of Women in Industry in the Department of Labour. The State League also did its share of work to attain a federal bill for the Regulation of the Meat Packing Industry, for a health insurance bill, and for the Sheppard-Towner bill.

In 1922, the New York State and New York City leagues were merged into one league: the Consumers' League of New York, with the office of the League in New York City, Mrs. Percy Jackson[1] being elected the first president.

---

[1] As this book goes to press, information has been received of the death of Mrs. Percy Jackson.

Among the many pamphlets published by the New York Consumers' League are: "Women's Wages To-day," "The Consumers' Coöperative Societies in New York State," "Behind the Scenes in a Hotel."

All mention of the work of the New York City League has been omitted from this state report, because the New York City League, having been the pioneer league, its work has been so closely linked up with the history of the movement that sufficient details have already been given in the body of the book.

NORTH CAROLINA

In 1913 a branch of the National Consumers' League was reported to have been formed in the State Normal School in Greensboro. There seems to be no other data available.

OHIO

One year after the National League was founded, the Consumers' League of Ohio was organized with headquarters in Cleveland (April, 1900), and six years later the Cincinnati League was started. A local league was formed in Canton in 1911 and functioned for a couple of years, but apparently had not sufficient vitality to live longer. However, the Toledo League, which did not appear in the field until sixteen years after the parent League was organized in Cleveland, has been, as well as the Cincinnati League, a tower of strength, doing valiant work. The Ohio League has also had the intelligent coöperation of the students of the Western Reserve University, one of whom, under the direction of the School of Applied Sciences of the

University, has recently made a study of the children who took out part-time and vacation working certificates.

The Ohio League, through its various local leagues, has accomplished much work; it has created an enlightened public opinion throughout the state, thus paving the way for legislation looking towards the betterment of industrial conditions.

It increased the demand for goods made and sold under right conditions to such an extent that manufacturers who had their plants in Ohio sent requests to the League to send investigators to inspect their premises, with the view of being permitted to use the League label. Within three years after the first League was organized twenty-two stores in Cleveland were carrying labelled goods, and eight of them were on the League's White List, showing that they conformed to the Standard of a Fair House. This White List was abandoned ten years later because none of the merchants was willing to raise the minimum wage above seven dollars a week, and the League felt that it could not conscientiously recommend stores where such low wages were paid.

Among the League's many activities may be mentioned the pressure brought upon merchants which resulted in the early closing of stores, even during the Christmas holiday season; the raising of the age of working boys and girls to sixteen; securing the passage of an ordinance which prohibited children under twelve from selling newspapers in the down-town districts; establishing the Saturday half holiday and the weekly half holiday for grocery clerks; helping to secure the first

Child Labour Law in the state; taking the initiative in securing legislation to regulate hours of labour for women, and for reducing them from fifty-four to fifty a week; bettering the sanitary conditions of soda fountains, restaurant kitchens, and neighbourhood stores. It made studies of clerks in retail stores, including drug clerks, of women workers in factories, home workers in the clothing industry, women employed in banks, railroads, insurance, and other offices, and those operating elevators. It also investigated hours and wages of charwomen in office buildings and women workers in hotels.

A unique piece of work which deserves mention in more detail was the establishment, in 1909, of a coöperative employment bureau for girls, which was a pioneer in this field. It was more than a mere employment agency, it was "a constructive social agency working towards the prevention of wasted lives, by making the most of youth's possibilities"; it not only placed workers, giving advice as to choice of occupation and encouraging minors to remain longer at school, but made trade investigations and coöperated with other agencies; it also maintained a directory of boarding places. It conducted a summer camp on Lake Erie, within commuting distance of Cleveland. During the summer of 1911, seven hundred and five girls visited this tent colony and enjoyed the lake breeze, paying only a dollar a week for a cot.

The League, through its experience in connection with the Bureau, was enabled to secure the passage of a bill regulating employment bureaus, and aided in establishing the present City-State Free Employment Bureau to which it turned over its work in 1914.

The League has coöperated with the Board of Education, Vocation Bureau, and State Industrial Commission in bringing about reforms, and during the war was prominent in the work of the Ohio Council of National Defense, the president of the Cleveland League serving as chairman of the Committee on Women in Industry in the Council.

Realizing that the industrial workers were the third line of defense, the soldiers depending upon them for equipment of every kind, the League showed the necessity of keeping workers in good condition, so that their output would not be lessened. The League was called upon to furnish speakers to explain the workers' point of view, and many employers sent to the League office for literature. The League was able to point out the fact that in England it was found wiser to retain a short working day in order to keep the output at a high mark.

The Public Library, at the League's request, displayed the best books on industrial questions; health talks were arranged for factories and cooking classes started, that working women might be taught which were the most nourishing foods and how to prepare them.

The League helped to prepare bills to keep women out of the dangerous trades, the freight yards, and night taxi service. However, the American public is fickle; after the Armistice, public interest in working women ceased, and many people objected to "stirring up" labour, for fear workers might get more and more de-

fiant and arbitrary. It was considered unwise to encourage discontent among workers (even when conditions obviously needed remedying), as it might lead to
strikes and the ruin of business. The ruin of the
workers' health, with the inevitable dire consequences
affecting future generations, was apparently unworthy
of consideration. It takes years of hammering to
convince a thoughtless public that when workers are
well treated profits increase and the entire community
benefits.

The League was obliged to put forth much effort to
educate the public to demand a bill to make the Women
in Industry Service a permanent bureau and to secure
a larger appropriation for the State Industrial Commission, in order to increase the number of factory
inspectors. Few people were apparently aware of the
fact that these offices existed.

The Toledo League joined a round table of twenty-
four state-wide organizations interested in working
women and, under the banner of the Ohio Council of
Women in Industry, started a campaign for a minimum
wage. Through the League's persuasion, Miss Mary
Anderson of the Woman's Bureau, United States
Labour Department, sent her experts to cover the
state and thus secured up-to-date statistics and data
on wages and living costs.

The League has become an authoritative source of
information for students of economics. At the present
time, when, through the work of the League, the public
conscience has become more sensitive, it is difficult to
credit the facts which appear in some of the League

reports. Until the Consumers' League focussed the attention of a careless shopping public on the consumers' responsibility for the existence of certain evils, no one gave a thought to little boys in knickerbockers delivering heavily framed pictures at half-past ten o'clock on Christmas Eve, or boxes of candy at twenty minutes past midnight, with more boxes to be delivered even at that cruelly late hour.

The Cincinnati League presented its cause in a picturesque and dramatic manner, through the medium of two original plays, written especially for it, one a comedy entitled: "Merry Christmas,"[1] giving the harassed shopper's point of view; the other a touching tragedy called: "The Shadowed Star,"[2] founded upon actual conditions which showed the hardships of overburdened workers at the holiday season. The first president of the Ohio Consumers' League was Miss Belle Sherwin, who served until 1903, when Mrs. Frederic C. Howe succeeded to the office. A few years later she was followed by Miss Myrta L. Jones, who served in that capacity many years. She became so identified with the work of the League, and was so assiduous in promoting its welfare, that in 1910 she was elected a vice-president of the National Consumers' League and has held that office ever since. At the present time, Miss Wilma C. Ball is president of the Ohio League, and Miss Jones has been elected honorary vice-president. Whatever may have been the results of the Ohio League's work, none has been more fruitful

---

[1]Written by Miss Elizabeth R. Kellogg.
[2]Written by Miss Mary Louise McMillan.

than the embedding in the hearts of the founders the firm faith in the righteousness of the cause, and the belief that an ever-widening circle will eventually wish to share in the working girls' heroic struggle for equity and justice. To quote a member of the Toledo League:[1] "The work has been a glory in the lives of those who were permitted through the League to understand better the noble aspirations of thousands of working women."

OREGON

In 1902, the president of the New York City League was invited to speak in Portland, Oregon, on the aims and work of the Consumers' League. The following year, 1903, the Consumers' League of Oregon appeared on the horizon, with Miss Mary Montgomery as its first president. Its first piece of work was to secure an amendment to the Ten-Hour Law for working women, so as to extend its protection to retail-store workers, these not having been included in the original bill. The amendment was passed in 1907, but the act carried exemption for one week preceding Christmas Day, thus enabling firms to employ women twelve hours a day during the holiday season. Two years later the League secured a further amendment to the law, abolishing this privilege.

The Oregon Consumers' League took the initiative in endeavouring to secure sanitary conditions in the preparation, distribution, and storage of food. The Oregon crusaders in the campaign, feeling that more could be

[1] Olive A. Colton.

accomplished through an organization, joined the Consumers' League and asked to be allowed to work as a "pure food committee." At that time, pure food was not mentioned in the constitution or by-laws of the National Consumers' League. The National Pure Food Bill was before Congress. The Oregon League appealed to the National Consumers' League to include pure food as one of its objects of attainment. This was voted upon favourably. The Pure Food Bill was passed and became operative in January, 1907. The following May an open meeting of the Oregon Consumers' League was held, with addresses by representatives of the Board of Health, City Health Officers, and the City Food Inspector, illustrated by culture plates of germs secured from food obtained in the open market and vigorously commented on by the speakers. The meeting was largely attended, and much interest was manifested in the movement. Shortly afterwards, a campaign for pure milk was inaugurated. The work progressed slowly, owing to the lack of coöperation on the part of the State Food and Dairy Commissioner, who had held office continuously for a period of twelve years.

The Dairymen's Association also opposed the Portland city ordinance relating to the inspection and maintenance of dairies and the regulation of the sale of milk and cream. Despite this opposition, the ordinance was passed. It was found during the summer of 1909 that deaths of children under two years of age from gastro-enteric diseases were greater per capita in Portland than in Chicago. As there was no excessive heat and the drinking water was pure, it was decided that impure milk contributed largely to these results, and statements to this effect were incorporated in many death certificates.

With the support of the Oregon *Daily Journal*, the campaign was pushed energetically. An article published August 29, 1909, stated: "Six hundred and eighteen babies less than a year old died in Portland last year, and tuberculous or dirty milk was the cause of nearly every death."

In response to a petition to the State Board of Health to take active measures to improve dairy conditions, the officials asked the League to arouse the public conscience to the end that the State Board of Health receive proper support in its efforts.

The League secured the coöperation of all organizations interested in public health: the Chamber of Commerce, Oregon Tuberculosis Association, Oregon branch of the National Health League, Visiting Nurses' Association, the women's clubs, the City and County Medical Society; and those associations bombarded the State Board of Health with petitions.

Members of the State and City Boards of Health made personal visits of inspection to dairies, under the auspices of the Pure Food Committee of the Consumers' League. The disclosures fully justified the reports made by the Oregon *Daily Journal* and emphasized the need of vigorous enforcement of the pure milk ordinance. A new ordinance was passed calling for two new inspectors, one to be a chemist and the other a veterinarian. Thus, tuberculin test of milk cows became effective

An appeal for advice was then sent to the United States Department of Animal Industry; veterinarians were sent to inspect herds throughout the state. The result of this inspection proved that infection was worse than in any other state. An appeal was then made to the Governor of the State and, as a result of an investigation of the office of the Pure Food and Dairy Commissioner, this officer was impeached by the Legislature for mismanagement of office, a deputy being appointed to fill his unexpired term. The Pure Food Committee went twice to the Capitol to give testimony. Statistics show that from 1909, when conditions were the worst, until 1914, improvement had been so marked that at the Panama Exposition, held in California, Oregon stood first in competition with the world for pure milk and dairy products.

Inquiries from all over the country, as well as from foreign countries, have been received by the Oregon Board of Health, in regard to proper methods to pursue. The development has steadily gone on. The value of the accomplishment may be seen at a glance by the following abstract from the report of the Chief Dairy and Milk Inspector:

Number of deaths under two years of age from diarrhœa and enteritis, starting with the year milk inspection began in Portland:

Year	No. Deaths	Rate per 1000 Births
1909	100	32.6
1910	73	21.5
1911	57	15.2
1912	38	9.3
1913	29	7.7
1914	15	3.6

Year	No. Deaths	Rate per 1000 Births
1915	14	3.4
1916	12	3.0
1917	33	8.2
1918	24	5.1
1919	26	9.5
1920	22	4.2
1921	19	3.5
1922	17	3.2

Thus it can be noted how readily consumers, when organized, can change conditions in their community. Instead of complacently permitting abuses, the source of evil must be discovered and abolished, and drastic measures pursued by conscientious citizens well organized, in order to bring about successful achievement. An awakened public conscience makes evil conditions unprofitable.

In 1913, the League secured the passage of a minimum-wage law, giving to the Industrial Welfare Commission jurisdiction, not only over wages, but also over hours and conditions of employment of women and minors. Since then, the various rulings of the Commission govern instead of the statutes.

The Industrial Welfare Commission is composed of three members, one representing the employers, one the employees, and the third, the public. The Commission set in motion machinery for formal conferences among the following groups: mercantile, manufacturing, laundry, restaurants, and office, all conferences being open to the public. At each conference there were three representatives of employers, three of employees, and three of the general public. Decisions of the

Industrial Welfare Commission were based on the recommendations made by each occupational group. One of the first results of the mercantile conferences was to close retail shops, in which women were employed, at 6 P. M. This applies only to the city of Portland; in the state at large 8.30 P. M. is the closing hour. This was an important achievement, as the League had been endeavouring unsuccessfully for several years to secure the coöperation of employers to effect a voluntary closing at that hour.

The chief variations in recommendations as to wages were due principally to the fact that women working in factories and laundries did not require as expensive clothing as women in offices or clerks in stores, who had contact with the public. In practically every case, recommendations were unanimous; the Commission called public hearings on the recommendations submitted and ultimately issued orders making the provisions obligatory.

In 1917, owing to the agitation on the part of the cannery interests and fruit growers, the ten-hour statute was amended, exempting from the jurisdiction of the Industrial Welfare Commission women employed in "harvesting, packing, curing, canning, or drying any variety of perishable fruit, vegetable, or fish for more than ten hours in one day." The Commission, however, secured a provision that when women were employed more than ten hours a day, they were to be paid time and a half for all overtime, and this clause protected the women from unduly long hours.

The legislation pertaining to the Industrial Welfare

Commission was attacked in the courts by a paper-box manufacturer of Portland, who claimed that it interfered with his constitutional rights. Assisted by the National Consumers' League the Oregon League successfully defended the suit and the law was upheld in the Oregon Supreme Court. The case was carried later to the United States Supreme Court. Mr. Louis Brandeis, who had previously (with the assistance of Miss Josephine Goldmark) prepared the brief showing the necessity of regulating women's wages in the interest of health and public welfare, had been appointed a Justice of the United States Supreme Court, so Mr. Felix Frankfurter appeared on behalf of the Consumers' League. The law was upheld by a majority decision of the Court. The Commission continued its work, in spite of opposition. At each successive legislature a lobby undertook to destroy its power, but without success.

The U. S. Department of Labour made a study of the results of minimum-wage legislation in Oregon, in which it was shown that the general standard of wages had been raised, women had not been replaced by men, and that industry had not been handicapped. As a proof that the Manufacturers' and Merchants' Association and the Laundry Owners' Association had found the minimum-wage commission beneficial, it must be noted that when the United States Supreme Court annulled the Minimum-Wage Law in the District of Columbia, they passed resolutions calling upon all their members to maintain the Oregon law then in effect, to obey the rulings of the Commission, and not to challenge the constitutionality of the law in the courts.

The Oregon League has taken an active part in child labour legislation and has been identified with campaigns conducted by other civic bodies, when the object of attainment coincided with the aims and principles of the League. Because of its conservative policy, its influence has been valued and its authority on industrial questions has met with the consideration which it merited.

PENNSYLVANIA

The first league to be organized after the New York League was the Consumers' League of Pennsylvania, which was formed nearly seven years later. A constitution was adopted and a governing board elected on February 28, 1897, and its first charter was granted about two years afterwards. When the Pittsburgh branch was formed in 1912, the charter was amended, its title being changed to the Consumers' League of Eastern Pennsylvania.

As the organization in eastern Pennsylvania grew in membership and consequent influence, the League's scope of work was gradually broadened. It made many investigations into the conditions of labour, trade, and industry, in order to enlighten the community and to suggest such changes as the public welfare warranted.

At first the League had volunteer investigators, but after the reorganization of the Department of Labour in 1913, the passage of the Woman's Labour Law, the Workmen's Compensation Act, and various other statutes, more skilled officials were going in and out of industrial establishments, so that the policy of the League has necessitated more and more the services of trained and experienced workers in research work and investigation.

The Eastern Pennsylvania League followed the example of the New York League by publishing the Standard of a Fair House and a White List, and by endeavouring to abolish overtime work on Saturdays and during the holiday season. By 1910, the League succeeded in securing the coöperation of all department-store firms, for they signed an agreement to close of an evening, not only at Christmas time, but throughout the year, each agreeing to close when all the others had signed. The League constantly coöperated with the National Consumers' League in creating a demand for goods bearing the White Label, and in holding exhibits of "Label" goods. It also took an active part in bringing about much-needed legislative reforms in regard to the protection of working women and children. It coöperated with the Women Workers' and Child Labour committees and assisted in preparing a bill which was passed in 1905 and known as the Factory Act. In 1913, a Woman's Labour Law was passed, limiting hours of labour to fifty-four a week, prohibiting night work, providing for lunch rooms, separate toilet facilities, seats in workrooms, pure drinking water, and a midday lunch period of forty-five minutes. The League was in a large measure responsible for the enactment of this law, as it was also for the pressure brought to reorganize the State Department of Labour and Industry. It has endeavoured, though unsuccessfully thus far, to establish the Civil Service system in this department and bring the department under its regulations. The League also introduced bills for minimum wage and an eight-hour working day, but up to this time these bills have not been passed. A representative of the League has been constantly on the watch, at every session of the State Legislature, fostering legislation in favour of better working conditions and opposing those detrimental to the interests of public welfare. During the stress of war, misguided employers endeavoured to nullify the Woman's Labour Law by asking for an abatement of the regulations in order to increase production. The National Consumers' League, however, having shown that in England the output of munitions was actually decreased by lengthening hours for workers, and increased when hours were again shortened, the Eastern Pennsylvania League was able, with the coöperation of other organizations, to prevent all modification or abatement of laws, in spite of a rising public sentiment owing to ignorance of facts.

The League has taken a prominent part in forwarding a movement for a woman's bureau in the Department of Labour and Industry, and in a campaign to demand competent appointees for official positions, but these goals have not yet been reached.

The League has coöperated with the Industrial Board of the State Department of Labour and Industry in suggesting rules and regulations for adequate protection of the life, health, safety, and morals of employees, notably in prohibiting the employment of messenger girls under twenty-one years of age.

The functions of the new Industrial Board, under the recent reorganization code of the state, are materially different from those of the former Board. In future, the Department of Labour will make all its own rules and regulations, and the Industrial Board will be merely advisory.

The League's advice was sought in relation to the preparation of the sanitary code, the laundry code, and the industrial home work code.

Realizing the futility of laws without proper enforcement, the League has been ever alert to aid in enforcement. When it had evidence of violations, it went directly to the employers concerned or else reported to the Department of Labour and Industry.

In 1910, a branch of the League known as the Industrial Betterment Bureau was started in coöperation with other social agencies in Philadelphia to investigate factory conditions and to supply a clearing house for labour by which workers may be diverted from less desirable to better conditions, also to supply workers to the employer in time of need. In 1912, an "after-care" committee was initiated in connection with the Bureau, with the idea of following up the industrial careers of applicants placed, and so to exert a beneficial influence on their industrial future. In 1915, this bureau was discontinued after the organization of a free employment bureau for adults under the control of the State Department of Labour and Industry. A placement bureau for children in the Bureau of Compulsory Education of the public schools was established. Partly as a result of the accumulation of facts relating to children, their trade opportunities and experiences, a movement for a trade school was started. The Consumers' League was represented on the committee fostering the movement.

In 1916, the League took a definite responsibility for the Bureau of Boarding Houses for Girls. Its aim was to maintain a registry of houses, inspected and supervised, where working women and girls without homes in the city might be provided with living quarters among decent surroundings, and to encourage the managers of these houses to maintain high moral and sanitary standards. This Bureau grew to such proportions that it became an independent organization in 1918, and later disbanded to reorganize under the auspices of the Y. W. C. A.

The Committee on Investigations, formed first to investigate the conditions in retail stores, soon broadened its activities to other fields of study and made general trade surveys as well as individual factory investigations. As early as 1907, it was realized that there was no general knowledge of conditions of women in industry in Philadelphia, so the Consumers' League determined to collect this material and make it available for general use. Studies were made and published of conditions in silk mills, hosiery mills, paper-box making, millinery, book binding, telephone service, and sweated industries, as well as the general living conditions and wages of Philadelphia working girls. A study of the wages and cost of living of women in department stores in Philadelphia was made under the auspices of the Department of Labour and Industry,

by Consumers' League investigators, and published as a
department document.

It has not been uncommon for industrial establishments and employing groups to make requests for
information which has entailed research, sometimes
of considerable importance. Two of these subjects:
"Some Philadelphia Firms Closed All Day Saturday,"
and "Vacations With Pay For Factory Workers,"
appear in the list of publications given below. An
immediate tangible result of the former compilation
was the closing on Saturdays in summer of the firm
making the inquiry and of the firm printing the findings.
Since the study was initiated many firms have adopted
the principle; therefore, it seems fair to assume that
their attention had been directed towards early closing
in summer by the publicity given to the report.

Some of the more recent reports published by the
Consumers' League, based on research, are:

Vacations with Pay for Factory Workers.
Industrial Home Work in Pennsylvania. (Done in
    conjunction with the Department of Labour and
    Industry and Bryn Mawr College).
Digest of State Labour Laws.
Trailing Behind, or How Pennsylvania Compares with
    Other States in Protective Legislation for Working
    Women and Children.
Coloured Women as Industrial Workers in Philadel-
    phia.
Some Philadelphia Firms Closed All Day Saturday.
Working Women and Children in Pennsylvania—An

Analysis of the Occupational and the Manufacturing Sections of the Fourteenth United States Census.

The Consumers' League has been represented on various state and municipal committees, and through its knowledge of facts has often been able to contribute valuable information. For instance, on the Fair Price Committee, in a campaign to buy cheaper cuts of meat, the League was able to prove that the packers were backing the movement for their own profit and not to reduce the high cost of living (as their representative had testified at a congressional hearing) and the whole matter was abandoned.

The Consumers' League, since its organization, has acted as a centre of information and maintains a library on subjects pertaining to women and children in industry and the laws and code rulings relating to them.

Through its educational platform it has been enabled to bring the pressure of a unified public opinion against many of the crying evils of the industrial system, and by so doing has benefited the consuming as well as the producing public.

It has been fortunate in having a devoted group of faithful and public-spirited women associated with its movement. Four officers and directors who served on the first governing board of the organization in 1897 still serve in official capacities. Mrs. Samuel S. Fels, Mrs. S. Burns Weston, Miss Anna C. Watmough, and Mrs. Walter Cope. To these names may be added those of Miss Florence Sanville, and Miss A. Estelle Lauder whose indefatigable work as executive secretaries for many years has been invaluable.

WESTERN PENNSYLVANIA

The Consumers' League of Western Pennsylvania, a member of the National League, was part of the State League, from its inception until 1912, at which time the Western Pennsylvania branch secured its own charter.

Before the charter was received and the State League was working for the passage of a child labour bill, the State League coöperated with the National Child Labour Association, and the western branch worked with the Allegheny County Child Labour Association, maintaining a secretary for the campaign.

For five years before the charter was received, and for two years afterwards, Mrs. William J. Askin was president.

The Western Pennsylvania branch has always followed the programme of the National League, so it has been active in all lines of legislation, both State and Federal.

When the White Label was in use, the best merchants of the city gave splended coöperation in having special public displays of White Label goods and in using the White Label stamp in advertising the annual sale of white goods.

In inaugurating the "Shop Early" campaign, the League offered prizes to high-school pupils for the best essays on "Early Christmas Shopping." The response was tremendous, and the task of reading and deciding was heavy.

The next step was to petition the banks to release the Christmas Savings fund two weeks earlier, that the rush might not come at the last minute.

The National Sweatshop Exhibit was displayed at the Pittsburgh Exposition.

The League put on an educational campaign by asking the clubs, especially those in the smaller towns, to have an Industrial Day on their programme, one member to prepare a paper on some subject pertaining to women and children in industry, the League sending literature on the subject, or suggesting a line of reading, this to be followed by an open discussion of the subject led by the secretary of the League. Abstracts of the law were distributed, with the request that violations be reported to the League, the League in turn reporting to the Department of Labour. This has been of great value, not only in checking violations, but when pressure is needed on State or Federal representatives, these clubs answer our call.

Our affiliation with the Congress of Clubs of this district affords many opportunities to spread the work.

The League has always worked in harmony with other organizations, has had good service from the Department of Labour, all reported violations having been taken care of and reported back to the League.

From the beginning the League has had the endorsement of the Chamber of Commerce.

Special speakers have been sent into the field in behalf of the Sheppard-Towner bill, the Child Labour amendment, and *against* the Equal Rights bill.

The National Consumers' League met in Pittsburgh

in 1911, the speakers being President John Graham
Brooks, Mrs. Frederick Nathan, First Vice-President,
Mrs. Florence Kelley, Secretary, Miss Florence Sanville,
Dr. John A. Ryan.

RHODE ISLAND

In December, 1901, the Rhode Island Council of
Women called a meeting in Pembroke Hall, Brown
University, to hear the president of the New York
City League give the theory and purpose of the Consumers' League. At the close of her address, the Rhode
Island Consumers' League was formed, with an initial
membership of forty-six; its purpose was declared to
be "the formation of public opinion which shall lead
consumers to recognize their responsibilities." The
following platform was adopted:

(1) All goods should be made under sanitary conditions for the protection of both worker and consumer.

(2) Good work should command adequate compensation.

(3) Employees should receive fair wages and humane
consideration.

In 1912, the membership increased to three hundred
and sixteen and the League was incorporated under the
laws of Rhode Island.

The first work undertaken by the League was to
create a popular demand for labelled goods through a
comprehension of the reasons for and use of the label.
The methods were the same as those employed by the
leagues of other states—investigation to see what
stores carried such goods, the advertising of the stores

and the goods, the endeavour to secure a varied line of labelled goods in as many shops as possible, and the arrangement of exhibits and sales of labelled goods. This work continued until the label was discontinued in 1918.

The next work of importance was for early Christmas shopping, now so universally established in principle and practice through the efforts of consumers' leagues throughout the country. For years the Consumers' League strove to induce people to shop early in December and early in the day. Then the editors of newspapers came to the League's assistance by running contests for the best cartoons on early Christmas shopping. Posters were placed in street cars and every conceivable means of advertising was used. In 1916, the Chamber of Commerce coöperated with the League in persuading the public to shop early. By 1919, the merchants, having realized the wisdom of the policy, undertook the advertising of the early shopping movement themselves.

The campaign for the six o'clock closing of stores was not so popular, nor has it been so universally accepted. The League endeavoured to induce firms to close at 6 P.M. during July and August, hoping thus gradually to extend the custom throughout the entire year. For several months, in 1914, many of the stores in Providence closed every night at six, including Saturday. Then the smaller specialty shops declined to follow the lead of the department stores, so because of competition, the latter were forced to reopen. The League, after making a study of the question, was able to show

that Saturday is not the universal pay-day, and therefore Saturday-evening shopping is not imperative. A
statement of facts relating to early closing was sent to
the Retail Merchants' Committee of the Chamber of
Commerce, which impressed the merchants to such a
degree that, by 1919, practically all the Providence
stores had adopted six o'clock closing every night in the
week. Only one large store is defying the general
practice, and that is one of a chain under New York
management. Providence has by no means been the
only place in the state where progress has been noticeable. In most of the other cities and in the larger
towns, it is only on Saturday evening that stores remain
open after six o'clock, but the new custom is spreading.
The merchants next considered the question of the
weekly half holiday to their employees during July
and August, and now this custom is in vogue in practically every large store in Providence. In 1923, one
firm gave, instead, a full holiday in the middle of the
week during these two months.

The League found that because retail stores were not
included under the Factory Act, which limited the
working hours of women and children, clerks in stores
were sometimes working as long as fourteen hours a
day. The League therefore set about having the provisions of the Fifty-four Hour Law (passed in 1913)
extended to include mercantile and business establishments. This was probably the greatest single achievement of the League during its early years.

The League has not been content merely to do
legislative work, it has also taken up law violations

with managers of stores, and if these were persisted in, they were reported to the State Inspection Department.

A committee on conditions surrounding employees made painstaking investigations, and through the committee's influence, individual establishments were improved; rest rooms were provided, an additional number of seats secured, as well as seats with backs, steel lockers for cloaks and hats installed, hospitals and fire drills organized, greater protection from fire assured, and better sanitary conditions inaugurated. These improvements which the committee was able to secure in certain stores were also obtained by the executive secretary in some of the factories.

As early as 1903, the League began to arouse interest in children engaged in industrial occupations, and secured the passage of laws prohibiting night work for those under sixteen years of age; nine years later an act prohibiting messengers under twenty-one from working after 10 P.M. was passed; and again, three years afterwards, a Street Trades bill placed further restrictions upon boys and girls under sixteen years of age. In 1923 the Children's bill was passed, which prohibited the employment of children on specified dangerous machinery and in certain hazardous occupations, required a standard physical examination for children about to enter industry, raised the age at which children can leave school for work from fourteen to fifteen, and provided for special certificates for children of fourteen to work when school is not in session.

It is generally conceded that practically all the

statutes for working children have been enacted through the League's influence.

Legislation for women has met with strong opposition because the state is industrial, and progress has therefore been slow. However, the League helped to secure the reduction of working hours for women and minors to fifty-four hours a week and ten hours a day, covering manufacturing, mechanical, mercantile, and business establishments without exception; secured the provision of seats for women employees, the prohibition of the common cup and towel in industry, and procured the abolition of the "Kiss of Death" shuttle in textile mills.

The Rhode Island League has had the true spirit of the pioneer in initiating movements and then turning over the work to the authorities to whom they properly belonged. The establishment of the Coöperative Employment Bureau may be cited as one example. Realizing that the city was doing little to help find the right kind of work for the boy or girl who must leave school early, the League, in 1912, coöperated with seven other civic organizations in order to give practical advice to these children and to help them obtain suitable positions. Again the Chamber of Commerce assisted, this time in convincing the Providence Public School authorities that the work rightfully belonged to them, and in 1918 it became the Bureau of Vocational Guidance, under the public school system.

A unique movement fostered by the Rhode Island League was the Governor Beeckman Prize Garden

Contest, which started in 1916. For years the League had felt the need of encouraging the operatives in the mill villages to raise their own vegetables and to surround their homes with flowers and shrubs. The state raised so little of its food that the matter was a vital economic one in regard to the operatives; for if food were costly and wages low, the result was in many cases undernourishment. Therefore, the Consumers' League asked the Rhode Island League of Improvement Societies to coöperate in this movement and sent a request to Governor Beeckman for prizes of silver cups to be given the operatives who developed the best flower gardens in the state. In order to retain the prizes permanently, they had to be won three years in succession, so an additional gift of ten dollars in gold was also awarded to the cup winners and five dollars in gold for the second-best gardens. A prize was also offered to the village which showed the greatest improvement during the spring and summer. The contest, carried on for four years, grew to such proportions that nearly four thousand gardens were inspected the last year. As the United States was at war and people all over the country were being urged to raise their own food stuffs, the contest gained in importance; it is, therefore, significant that in 1918 more than five hundred operatives received certificates of achievement signed by the Governor for having substantially increased the production of food.

The League has never undertaken any new work without first pursuing a scientific investigation; as many as five such investigations have been carried on in one year.

One of the strongest features of the League's work has been the education of the public through membership campaigns, lectures, distribution of literature on subjects of particular interest, and generally spreading the knowledge of the League's purposes and ideals.

For six years the League held prize contests in the public and private schools for the best essay on some phase of the League's work.

Two other interesting experiments were successfully tried. In 1919, a public course of lectures on economics was held at a central meeting place. The League also formed a committee of twenty-one, representing capital, labour, and the public, to meet together in order to discuss frankly the controversial problems which so frequently caused friction between capital and labour, as well as seriously inconvenienced the consuming public.

It can readily be seen that investigation, education, and legislation are the established principles of all consumers' leagues.

In Rhode Island other organizations have been so convinced, through the propaganda of the Consumers' League, of the responsibility of each and every member of society for the conditions under which the articles they consume are made and distributed, that they all now have committees on women in industry and on child labour or child welfare. It is, therefore, difficult to measure accurately the results of the work of the Consumers' League. Without doubt its influence in shaping the policies of the state affecting women and children in industry has been and will continue to be a momentous factor.

TENNESSEE: 1903-12

During the first two years of its existence the Tennessee League distributed a quantity of literature, and among the women's clubs it strove to stimulate discussion of such topics as child labour, tenement home work, and other subjects pertaining to the work of the National Consumers' League.   In Knoxville, it conducted a campaign for labelled garments and early Christmas shopping.   Mrs. Joel C. Tyler was the president of the League.

TEXAS: 1913-20

A local branch was organized in Austin, and through its efforts a minimum-wage commission was temporarily established.   However, it seemed impossible to secure reasonable wages for the mixed classes of white, coloured, and Mexican working women and girls, and so the task was abandoned.

UTAH: 1903-05

No data apparently available.

VERMONT: 1903-07

Two branches were organized—one in Burlington and one in St. Johnsbury—but there seem to be no reports of work accomplished.

VIRGINIA: 1901–02

This league apparently died in its infancy.

WISCONSIN

The Consumers' League of Wisconsin was organized more than seventeen years ago. Under the leadership of Mrs. B. C. Gudden of Oshkosh, it established a programme of work that has been continuous in its activities to the present day. During the first years, the emphasis was placed upon the work of educating the public in order that the demand be created for goods manufactured under conditions favourable to the workers. After the public conscience had been aroused, the next step was to secure adequate protective legislation for workers. For the last six or eight years the Consumers' League of Wisconsin has interested itself almost exclusively in efforts to secure legislation promoting the welfare of women and children in industry.

The League has initiated the following legislative programme by preparing the bills, attending the hearings, and lobbying for their passage:

(1) Minimum-Wage Law, which was passed and was in effect when the League conducted a second investigation in order that the wage be raised. An increase in the wage was secured.

(2) A bill asking that no child be given a permit to work until he was fourteen years of age and had finished the eighth grade in school or else completed nine years outside of kindergarten. This was passed and is now a law.

(3) A bill to include girls working in hotels, under the State Fifty-five Hour Law, and also the supervision of the Industrial Commission as to hours and wages. This bill was defeated three times, but finally passed in 1922.

The League has also prepared petitions to the Industrial Commission asking that:

(1) Night work be abolished in factories. This request was granted.

(2) The eight-hour day be given. This latter has never been directly granted. Hence the law now is fifty hours a week.

(3) A petition was submitted to the Supreme Court asking for a rehearing of the case which caused a decision to be rendered taking from the Industrial Commission all power to regulate women's hours of labour. The Court reversed its decision after securing the facts as submitted in the brief which accompanied the petition. This was done without a rehearing.

The results of two minimum-wage investigations conducted by the League have been published in pamphlet form. A report of an investigator, secured by the League, on conditions in Wisconsin hotels, was published in the *Survey* and reprints used in the 1922 Legislation.

A Summary of Protective Laws for the Working Women and Children of Wisconsin was published. Librarians have sent for this summary and it has found its way into twenty-eight different states of the Union.

APPENDIX H

Form of Agreement Between the National Consumers' League and the Manufacturers

THIS AGREEMENT, made this   day of   in the year   , between the NATIONAL CONSUMERS' LEAGUE, party of the first part, hereinafter referred to as LEAGUE, and   of the City of   County of   State of   party of the second part, hereinafter referred to as MANUFACTURER

Witnesseth, Whereas, the aforesaid League has been organized for the purpose of promoting intelligent and effective coöperation among the purchasers in demanding goods made under right conditions in preference to the Sweat Shop product;

And Whereas, the said League has adopted the following label:

which is registered to distinguish in the market goods made under conditions in respect to age of employees, hours of labour, and provisions for health and safety approved by it;

And Whereas, the parties of the first part are appointed with full power to allow to manufacturers the use of said label;

And Whereas, the said League is broadly advertising to the public the use and significance of the aforesaid label;

And Whereas, said Manufacturer is conducting his factory under conditions that have been investigated and approved by said League, and is desirous of securing whatever benefits there are to be derived by using the aforesaid label on goods made in said Manufacturer's premises—

Now, Therefore, in consideration of the sum of $1.00 and the covenants contained herein, it is mutually agreed as follows:

1st. That this Agreement is numbered , and that each and every one of the aforesaid labels used by the said Manufacturer shall be marked License Number

2d. That the said League will furnish without charge to said Manufacturer three electrotypes of each of the several sizes of the aforesaid label that are required by said Manufacturer for the various goods on which they are to be used.

3d. That the said Manufacturer, at his own expense, shall provide such duplicates of said electrotypes as are needed for making rubber stamps or for printing labels, and that all expenses for said labels shall be borne by said Manufacturer, and that said labels shall be attached in a manner approved by the League to garments made by such Manufacturer.

4th. That said Manufacturer will not during the continuance of this Agreement, or any time thereafter, furnish the aforesaid label to any other party.

5th. That said Manufacturer agrees to maintain said factory under conditions approved by said League, among which conditions the following are especially agreed to, viz.:

1. That all provisions of the State Factory Law and rulings of the State Wage Commission are to be complied with.

2. That the label is to be used by said Manufacturer only when all stitched goods, sold by the Manufacturer, are made on premises previously approved by the League.

(a) Said Manufacturer agrees to furnish said League with addresses of all premises where any part or parts of stitched goods sold by him are made.

(b) Said Manufacturer furthermore agrees that no stitched goods nor any part thereof be manufactured, altered or repaired in a room or apartment any part of which is used as a dwelling, nor in any room directly connected therewith.

3. (a) That standards approved by the League with regard to cleanliness, sanitation, lighting and ventilation shall be maintained on the premises at all times.

(b) That such physical conditions shall be maintained on premises as will not give rise to fire, and will minimize the spread of fire, and that safe egress shall be provided to accommodate all workers.

4. That no girl under the age of sixteen years

shall be employed, or permitted or suffered to work on such premises.

5. That no female shall be employed, or suffered or permitted to work in said factory between the hours of 10 P. M. and 7 A. M., nor longer than nine hours in any one day, except for the purpose of making one shorter work day, in which case the hours shall not exceed ten in any one day, nor fifty-four hours in any one week.

6. (a) That entrance to the premises for purposes of inspection shall be granted at any time to the League's accredited investigator.

(b) That all records of hours and wages shall be accessible to any investigator duly accredited by the League, no information so gathered to be made public in so far as it involves the name of the individual firm.

7. That said Manufacturer shall immediately notify said League if a strike or lockout occur in his factory, it being understood that the League reserves the right to suspend the use of its label during such strike or lockout.

6th. The license hereby granted to the Manufacturer by the League may be revoked by the League whenever in its opinion the Manufacturer has violated any of the conditions of this agreement or whenever, for any reason or cause, the League desires such revocation. Written notice of such revocation of license shall be given by registered mail to the Manufacturer at the address given below, and all rights of the Manufacturer to use the label shall terminate thirty days after his receipt of such notice.

In case of revocation the Manufacturer hereby agrees—

1. To return immediately all electrotypes of the League label in his possession or under his control, whether the same have been furnished to him by the League or otherwise procured.

2. To destroy or return to the League at its election all labels which the Manufacturer then has on hand.

3. To discontinue forthwith using said labels or attaching same to any goods manufactured or in process of manufacture, or to any boxes, packages, stationery, or advertising matter of any kind.

Should the use of said label be thus discontinued, said Manufacturer shall have the right to dispose of such goods as may be in stock in case said label cannot be removed without injuring the appearance of the goods.

7th. In the event of the failure of the Manufacturer to comply forthwith with all of the above conditions, upon receipt of notice of revocation as aforesaid, the said Manufacturer agrees to pay within thirty days as liquidated damages to said League or its authorized agent the sum of One Hundred Dollars ($100.00) without prejudice of the right of said League to enjoin the further use of said label by said Manufacturer. The said Manufacturer further agrees to pay as liquidated damages for any violation by him of the factory maintenance conditions above specified in Paragraph Fifth, the sum of One Hundred Dollars ($100.00) for each failure to comply with said conditions.

8th. This agreement may be terminated by either party by his giving to the other party by registered mail thirty days' notice of his intention to terminate the same.

In Witness Whereof, the said League has hereunto set its hand and seal to this and to another instrument of like tenor and date, by   , its President, and   , its Treasurer, and said Manufacturer by in the day and year as above written.

_____   _____
Witness for   *President of League.*

_____   _____
Witness for   *Treasurer of League.*

_____   _____
Witness for   *Representative of Manufacturer.*

                                       _____
                                       Address of Manufacturer.

APPENDIX I

First Published List of Manufacturers Using the White Label of the National Consumers' League

George Frost Mfg. Co., Boston, Mass.
Worcester Corset Co., Worcester, Mass.
C. F. Hathaway & Co., Waterville, Me.
Wm. T. Burns Underwear Co., Worcester, Mass.
Fairmount Mfg. Co., Hyde Park, Mass.

Whitall Mfg. Co., Lowell, Mass.
Westboro Underwear Co., Westboro, Mass.
Israel Underwear Co., Worcester, Mass.
Natick Underwear Co., Springfield, Mass.
Keach & Brown, Valley Falls, R. I.
E. A. King, Valley Falls, R. I.
Cummings Mfg. Co., Philadelphia, Pa.
Samuel A. Murray, Jr., Philadelphia, Pa.
Jackson Corset Co., Jackson, Mich.
Paul, Enochs & Co., Philadelphia, Pa.

APPENDIX J

First Published List of the Officers of La Ligue Sociale
d'Acheteurs of France

Mme. Klobb, President.
Mme. Georges Brincard, Vice-President.
Mme. L. de Contenson, Vice-President.
Mme. Jean Brunhes, General Secretary, Hôtel des
   Sociétés Savantes, 28 Rue Serpente (Bureau de la
   Ligue).
M. J. Bergeron, Assistant Secretary.
Prof. Jean Brunhes, Assistant Secretary

APPENDIX K

First Published List of the Officers and Advisory Board
of Der Sozialen Kaüferliga of Switzerland, 1906

Mme. E. Pieczynska-Reichenbach, Berne.
Herr und Frau Jean Brunhes, Fribourg.

Fräulein H. von Mulinen, Berne.
Fräulein F. Schmid, Berne.
Frau M. Adam, Berne.
Fräulein A. von Rodt, Berne.
Fräulein M. Gabot, Berne.
Frau M. Von Steiger, Berne.
Fräulein A. Stettier, Berne.
Herr Filliol, Berne.

Corresponding Advisory Board

Fraulein Mathilde Koller, Zurich.
Herr Dr. A. Joos, Basle.
Mme. Eugène Pittard, Geneva.
Mlle. Rachel de La Rive, Geneva.
Mme. Pierre Bovet, Nuremburg.
M. le professeur Clerget, Fribourg.
Fräulein Julia Rothpletz, Aarau.
Frau Dr. Faas, Berne.
Frau Dora Elchfeld, St. Gallen.

APPENDIX L

First Published List of the Officers of Der Liga von
Konsumenten of Germany, 1905

President: Frau Staatsminister von Bethmann-Hollweg,
Exzellenz.
First Vice-President: Elizabeth von Knebel-Doeberitz.
Second Vice-President: Prof. Dr. Ernst Franke.
Secretary: Martha Meinecke.
Assistant Secretary: Dr. Heinrich Koch.

Treasurers: Adele Beerenson.
Else Lueders.

Business Office: Nollendorfstr 29–30.

The Consumers' League of Holland,
Officers and Directors, 1903.

President: T. Sanders, V. Zeghenstraat, 78, Amsterdam.
Secretary: H. S. Veldman, 20 Vloesdÿk, Kampen.
Mr. P. A. Nicolaas, 30 Weteringstraat, Amsterdam.
Mr. J. Zody, Moddermolenstug, Amsterdam.
Mr. D. deClereq, Bloemendaal, Haarlem
Miss H. W. Crommelin, 21 Drift, Utrecht.
Miss H. Bahlmaun, Bussum.
Mr. H. Luken Jr., Zwolle.
Mr. J. Huizinga, 8 Veenestraat, Kampen.

APPENDIX M

Resolutions (Freely Translated) Passed at the First
International Conference of Consumers' Leagues,
Geneva, Switzerland, 1908

Overtime Work

Whereas, overtime work at night is a cause of the utmost physical and moral wretchedness,
RESOLVED, that consumers be requested never to give an order without first stipulating that no overtime work be permitted.
Whereas, all should strive persistently for the complete abolition of overtime work at night,

RESOLVED, that this conference affirms
1. That in labour laws lies the surest hope of improvement,
2. That the liberty of working people should be safeguarded against all unjust demands for overtime.

Bills

RESOLVED, that the members of the Consumers' Leagues should be absolutely prompt and scrupulous in the payment of bills when rendered.

RESOLVED, that consumers shall as soon as possible be enabled to recognize, by means of a label, goods made under wholesome social conditions.

RESOLVED, that consumers neglect no opportunity to be of service in the conflicts which continually arise between employers and employees.

RESOLVED, that trade-union groups of home-workers be developed increasingly; that investigations of home work be conducted, and exhibits be held from time to time; and that legislation be enacted to control home work.

RESOLVED, that Consumers' Leagues in all countries where there is no law regarding seats shall conduct a legislative campaign on this subject, and in all countries which have this law, shall keep watch that saleswomen are allowed to use seats.

RESOLVED, that the first International Conference of Consumers' Leagues, moved by the revelations of the recent investigations of the method of recruiting workers for the cocoa plantations at St. Thomas and Principi, protest against the continuation of such slavery.

RESOLVED, that all the chocolate manufacturers who buy from St. Thomas, even in small quantities, should join the English and German manufacturers in their effort to suppress the existing evils.

APPENDIX N

First Published List of the Provisional Committee of La Ligue Sociale d'Acheteurs of Belgium, 1910

MM. Le Baron Felix de Bethune
Prof. Adolphe Buyssens
Mlle. Ch. Ruegger
Mme. Van Vliet
Mlle. Emma Koenig

APPENDIX O

White List Standard for Laundries

Wages

(1) Equal pay is given for equal work irrespective of sex, and no woman who is eighteen years of age or over and who has had one year's experience receives less than $6 per week. This standard includes piece workers.

(2) Wages are paid by the week.

(3) Wages must be paid not more than twenty-four hours after a demand by the worker.

Hours

(1) The normal working week does not exceed fifty-four hours, and on no day shall work continue after 9 P. M. or for more than ten hours.

(2) When working after 7 P. M., twenty minutes is allowed for supper and supper money is given.

(3) A half holiday in each week during two summer months.

(4) A vacation of not less than one week with pay is given during the summer season.

(5) All overtime work beyond the fifty-four hours a week standard is paid for.

(6) Wages paid and premises closed on the six legal holidays, viz.: Thanksgiving Day, Christmas Day, New Year's Day, the Fourth of July, Decoration Day, and Labour Day.

Physical Conditions

(1) Washrooms are either separated from other workrooms or else adequately ventilated so that the presence of steam throughout the laundry is prevented.

(2) Work and retiring rooms are apart from each other and conform in all respects to the present Sanitary Laws.

(3) All machinery is adequately guarded.

(4) Proper drains under washing and starching machines, so that there are no wet floors.

(5) Seats adapted and adjusted to the machines are provided for:

a. Collar ironer feeder.
b. " " catcher.
c. " dampener feeder.
d. " " catcher.
e. " straightener.
f. " starch feeder.
g. " " catcher.
h. Handkerchief flat-work feeder and catcher.
i. Folders on small work.
j. Collar shaper.
k. " seam dampener.
l. Straight collar shaper.
m. And all other machines wherever possible.

(6) Humane and considerate behaviour toward employees is the rule.

(7) Fidelity and length of service meet with the consideration which is their due.

(8) The ordinances of the city and the laws of the state are obeyed in all particulars.

THE END

INDEX

INDEX

239

*For Product Safety Concerns and Information please contact
our EU representative GPSR@taylorandfrancis.com Taylor & Francis
Verlag GmbH, Kaufingerstraße 24, 80331 München, Germany*

T - #0132 - 230425 - C1 - 205/140/13 [15] - CB - 9780367194789 - Gloss Lamination